Kevin,

When you finish this book you'll know almost as much as I do about the Indians. Use it in good health.

Merry Christmas

[illegible]

Other Books By Terry Pluto

- Falling from Grace: Can Pro Basketball Be Saved?
- The Curse of Rocky Colavito
- Tall Tales: The Glory Years of the NBA
- Loose Balls: The Short, Wild Life of the American Basketball Association
- Bull Session (with Johnny Kerr)
- Tark (with Jerry Tarkanian)
- Forty-Eight Minutes: A Night in the Life of the N.B.A. (with Bob Ryan)
- Sixty-One: The Season, the Record, the Men (with Tony Kubek)
- You Could Argue but You'd Be Wrong (with Pete Franklin)
- A Baseball Winter (with Jeff Neuman)
- Weaver on Strategy (with Earl Weaver)
- The Earl of Baltimore
- Super Joe (with Joe Charboneau and Burt Graeff)
- The Greatest Summer

Burying the Curse

How the Indians Became the Best Team in Baseball

By Terry Pluto

Published by the Akron Beacon Journal

The Beacon Journal Publishing Company
44 East Exchange Street
Akron, Ohio 44328

Library of Congress Catalog Card Number: 95-83184

ISBN 0-9649902-3-7

Printed in the United States of America

10 9 8 7 6 5 4 3 2 1

To Frank Voss and Frank Sarmir, two good friends.
We grew up with the Indians.

Acknowledgments

The Beacon Journal has never published a book quite like this before. In order to make it happen, a number of people went beyond the call of duty. The decision to pull the trigger on this project was made by Publisher John Dotson, Editor Dale Allen and Managing Editor Glenn Guzzo. It was a gusty decision on their part because very few newspapers have ever undertaken a project quite like this.

In general, writers have little use for editors. They tend to make a writer's job harder, but I was blessed to be teamed with Ann Sheldon Mezger. I can never thank her enough for her patience and her eye for details. The manuscript also received careful readings from Roger Mezger and Roberta Pluto.

The cover illustration was created by artist John Backderf, who also did the type design for the cover and title page and the layouts for the pictures taken by Beacon Journal staff photographers.

Art Krummel, the Beacon Journal's publishing systems manager, designed the pages of text, coordinated with the printer, and did the computer programming necessary to get this book quickly into print.

The Beacon Journal's library staff, in particular Diane Leeders, was especially helpful.

Finally, John Hart, Mike Hargrove and Dan O'Dowd of the Indians were very helpful all season, giving me their time and insight.

— Terry Pluto

Acknowledgments

CONTENTS

1

WHAT'S WORTH REMEMBERING

The pitcher is from Nicaragua, the catcher from the Dominican Republic. The greyhound centerfielder is from the projects of East Chicago, Ind., and the strong, sometimes sullen leftfielder is from Shreveport, La. Their boss is from the dusty Texas panhandle.

I am talking about the manager and players who helped deliver the first World Series to Indians baseball fans in 41 years. I am talking about guys from Latin America and from the American South. Some of them are black, others are white, and a lot of them are Hispanic.

I am talking about men who probably wouldn't spend five minutes with each other if they all didn't happen to play baseball with the Cleveland Indians.

But they lived together for six months, almost like a Martin Luther King Dream Team — a group of folks of different races and backgrounds working together for a common goal.

I thought about this as the Indians did something I never thought I'd see. They won the American League pennant. They did it in the Seattle Kingdome, and that seemed a little strange because Seattle wasn't even in the major leagues when I first came to love the Indians. They did it with Dennis Martinez on the mound, and I never expected Dennis to pitch for the Tribe, either. We first met in 1979, when Martinez was a 23-year-old pitcher for the Baltimore Orioles and I was a 23-year old baseball writer for the Baltimore Evening Sun. He loved to make fun of me because he knew I was an Indians fan.

"Pluto, that team never wins anything," he said.

He was so right. From 1960 to 1993, the Indians never finished higher than third place, never nearer than 11 games behind in any season that wasn't interrupted by a strike. Boston fans always talked about the heartbreak of following their Red Sox, but we in northern Ohio only got heartburn from the Tribe. There was Ten-Cent Beer Night and the riot that ensued. There was the time the Indians gave out deodorant on Mother's Day; what a way to show Mom that you cared! I thought of all the old Cleveland jokes and of how the Indians played right into that depressing image of the city.

And I thought about how all of that had changed as I watched Dennis Jose Martinez of Granada, Nicaragua, beat Seattle, 4-0, in Game 6 of the American League Championship Series and send the team to a World Series.

The Curse of Rocky Colavito had been buried early in the 1995 season. I'm not exactly sure when it happened. I just know that there was a point when even the most jaded baseball fans among us realized that the 1995 Cleveland Indians were a great baseball team — a team the like of which we had never seen — and now it was our turn to get up to speed and to get with the program.

So much had happened during the regular season.

The Indians had won 100 games, more than any other team in big-league baseball. They did it in a 144-game season, with 18 games fewer than normally are scheduled. Along with Cal Ripken Jr., the Indians were one of the main reasons that many fans returned to baseball after the strike.

Sure, I loved how the Indians won 27 games in their last at-bat. I loved Albert Belle's relentless quest for greatness. First he wanted to beat Al Rosen's team record of 43 homers in 1953. Then he wanted to hit 50.

He did both. He hit more homers than any Indian ever, including two of my heroes — Rocky Colavito and Andre Thornton.

It was a year when Eddie Murray — another player whom I knew from the Orioles back in 1979 and whom I never expected to see in a Cleveland uniform — rapped out his 3,000th hit. He became a favorite of Tribe fans, who chanted "ED-DEE, ED-DEE" whenever the 39-year-old slugger came to bat. The fans nearly shook Jacobs Field when the numbers on the banner in left field changed with each hit that closed in on that 3,000 milestone.

Orel Hershiser won 16 games. So did Charles Nagy. Six Indians were All-Stars: Manny Ramirez, Kenny Lofton, Carlos Baerga, Belle, Martinez and Jose Mesa.

The biggest surprise was Mesa, who led the American League with 46 saves and set a major league record with 38 in a row. This from a guy who came into the season with a grand total of two big-league saves.

Mesa's success reminded me of the stories my father had told me about Gene Bearden. In 1948, Bearden was a 27-year-old lefty whose career had been spent in the minors. He had a knuckleball, and Tribe Manager Lou Boudreau was intrigued by the idea of a left-handed knuckleballer — the rarest of all pitchers, since knuckleballers are a unique breed even when they throw with the right arm. Anyway, Bearden pitched so well in spring training that he earned a spot in the starting rotation. This guy, who had never won a big-league game before, went out and became a 20-game winner for the 1948 Indians. He won Game 3 of the 1948 World Series and then came back in relief to save Game 6 and bring the world title to Cleveland.

In fact, Bearden was the last Tribe pitcher to save a post-season game until Mesa did it in 1995.

The sad part of the story is that after 1948, Bearden could not entice his knuckleball to dance in the strike zone. He threw wild and then lost confidence in the fickle pitch. He never won more than eight games in any season again and was out of baseball after 1953.

Hopefully, the Mesa story will be different. Mesa is pure heat — his 98 mph fastball could never be considered a Bearden-like gimmick. But it also is true that Jose Mesa never made an All-Star team anywhere until the 1995 season with the Indians. He was the wild card who became a bullpen ace, the man who pushed the Indians out of the ranks of the contenders and made them a team that won the Central Division by a record 30 games.

It seems so weird but so wonderful to say that: The Indians won their division by 30 games.

Heck, no baseball team ever had won any league or division by such a margin.

For Tribe fans, it wasn't a pennant race. It was a coronation and a celebration. It was a purging of demons and curses from the past.

That was what happened on Sept. 8, 1995, when the Indians clinched the Central Division title. Hershiser beat the Orioles, 3-2. The players raised championship banners, wore championship caps and T-shirts and paraded around the park after the game to a standing ovation from the sellout crowd of 41,656. There was champagne in the dressing room. There were tears of happiness and tears for tragedies past — especially when Garth Brooks' song, *The Dance*, was played after the game. *The Dance* had been the favorite song of Steve Olin, the Indians pitcher who was killed in a boating accident during the spring of 1993.

On the night of Sept. 8, 1995, every Indians player and fan had a special memory. Maybe it was a memory of the first Tribe player to give them an autograph. In my case, that was Mudcat Grant. Maybe it was a memory of the first player who made them care about the Indians. For me, that was Colavito. Maybe it was a memory of just having survived all the bleak years, as was the case for Manager Mike Hargrove, who played and managed in Cleveland when everything was not sellouts and applause.

Something else came to me as I watched the 1995 Indians.

We live in an age of rage. It is an age of Rodney King, O.J. Simpson and people extending a hand to someone from another background only if that hand goes around the neck. That is why it was so satisfying to see all these players covering every color of the human rainbow jumping, hugging, pouring champagne and celebrating what they have in common — rather than dwelling on what could easily have driven them apart.

It's good for our children to see this. It's important for them to know that Kenny Lofton, a city kid from East Chicago, can work between Albert Belle, a fellow African-American from Shreveport, and Manny Ramirez, a Dominican by way of New York City. And it's Lofton's job in the outfield to cover for both of them.

It does say something when a white pitcher who attended Bowling Green State University in Ohio can throw to a catcher from Puerto Rico by the name of Santos Valazquez Alomar Jr. — and the pitcher trusts the catcher to make the big decisions about the pitches.

The pitcher is Orel Hershiser. He became the Most Valuable Player of the 1995 American League playoffs, and he'll tell you that he loves how Sandy Alomar calls a game. He appreciates Alomar's physical talent and his brains.

The American League playoff clincher was pitched by Dennis Martinez, the reformed alcoholic from Nicaragua. His catcher was Tony Pena, who came from a farm in the Dominican Republic. The man who saved the game — Mesa — also came from a rural area of the Dominican Republic.

And all these guys won a pennant for Cleveland, Ohio.

This is not meant to romanticize the 1995 Cleveland Indians. They could be a hostile, surly group. There were days when Belle didn't just clam up with the press or fans — he barely said a word to his teammates. It was known as Albert Having One Of Those Days, and those who worked with him gave him a wide berth.

Murray could give you a stare that would crumble Mount Rushmore, and there were times when the players knew it wasn't wise to mess with

Eddie.

Lofton could be so suspicious of strangers — and even of his bosses — that it bordered on paranoia.

Jim Thome was well-meaning, but his Hayseed Kid From Peoria Act occasionally wore thin because he could seem so dense about things. Thome was the one who thought it was only a two-hour drive from Cleveland to Toronto. And it was Thome who talked about how, when he was a child, he put the family's pet rabbit in a blender. He wanted to make "a bunny drink." Luckily, Thome's mother rescued the hare before her son could flip the switch.

In the Tribe dressing room, the large contingent of Latin players chattered in Spanish, sometimes making the Americans feel a bit left out. The black players sometimes stayed in their own corner. The white players actually were a minority on this team. Of the 25 players on the post-season roster, only 10 of them were white.

I know that because I pulled out the roster and counted. I hadn't thought about it before; it hadn't mattered. Most Tribe fans didn't worry about the racial composition of the 1995 Indians. All they cared about was whether the team could play ball.

But the fact that so many guys from such different backgrounds did commit to winning and to each other says something special about the Indians — and their manager. Dudley Michael Hargrove saw very few folks like his players when he was growing up in Perryton, Texas.

"But Mike Hargrove is a very decent man with a good heart," said Andre Thornton, a former Tribe teammate of Hargrove's in the 1980s. "If Mike didn't treat all the different people fairly and if he had hypocrisy in his heart, the players would know it. They wouldn't hold together like they did."

If the players didn't respect each other and the manager, it might have led to a clubhouse war.

The Latin players wanted salsa music on the clubhouse stereo. Most of the blacks wanted rap. Some of the whites tried for country.

These guys weren't thrilled when one group hogged the music. But at least they didn't end up in a wrestling match as did former Indians Rick Sutcliffe and Broderick Perkins. Back in 1983, Sutcliffe wanted country music, Perkins pushed for soul, and then Perkins pushed Sutcliffe. It took four players to separate the two, as this fight was about far more than music.

Think about your office, your classroom, or any place where you rub against people who are foreign to you. Think about how easy it is for a simple, honest misunderstanding to ignite into something very ugly — something that strikes at the dark side of the human heart.

People who have been in sports and in the military will tell you that both are great equalizers. People from everywhere are tossed together.

In the military, getting along can be a life-and-death matter. It can be crucial to getting a squad through boot camp and out of maneuvers with everyone's health and sanity intact.

That happens in a ballgame, too. The passion to win must take precedence over racial prejudices. Team members have to rely on each other. They have to learn to count on the person next to them even though he may look different, talk different and maybe even think different.

That's true for the Indians and for any other successful athletic team.

The 1995 Indians didn't love one another, but they came to accept each other. If there is something worth leaving our children from this 1995 season — besides the lore and legend of a great baseball team — it is this: how these guys got along.

But a lot of dues had to be paid and changes had to be made before the Indians reached that stage.

2

THE SEASON FOR TEARS

Two years before they raised their first pennant since 1954, the Indians were a team cloaked in black. The year was 1993, and it is worth remembering what happened to this baseball team that spring.

Many of the fans who recently came to the Indians have never heard of Little Lake Nellie. If they recall anything at all about Tim Crews or Steve Olin, it is that they were a couple of Indians pitchers who died in some kind of accident.

These new Tribe fans say, "Hey, that's too bad and everything, but life goes on, right?"

Yes, life does indeed march on, often in remarkable ways. Since the Indians are winners now and since Jose Mesa became the kind of reliever Olin probably never would have been — well, why dig up the bones?

Why? Because that boating accident in the spring of 1993 on Little Lake Nellie near Clermont in central Florida tells you so much about this team and its manager. Out of respect to the families, published details of the accident were kept from being too specific. But Olin was nearly decapitated and Crews' body was crushed as he piloted the 18-foot, 150-horsepower boat into a dock at dusk. Supposedly, the throttle stuck and Crews couldn't stop the boat in time. If Bobby Ojeda had not been leaning forward a few inches, the top of his head would have been sliced off. As it was, doctors were able to repair and stitch up his sheared scalp, but they never could put together the psyche of a guy who was one of the most gritty and competitive pitchers in the game.

After a real brush with life-and-death, it was hard for Ojeda to give that same gravity to a baseball game. That was what he learned when he returned to the Indians late in 1993, pitched a few times, and then sort of drifted away. He felt like a ghost in the dressing room. He was The One Who Survived, and he really didn't know why. Why him? Why not Crews or Olin? It is impossible for any of us to know what demons haunted Ojeda in the dead of night.

And Manager Mike Hargrove? Nothing in his baseball career had prepared him for this. He and his wife Sharon had to become big brother and sister to some players, counselors to others. Yes, the Indians brought in professionals to help the living cope with the dead, but ballplayers are very suspicious of those they call "shrinks . . . head doctors . . . witch doctors." For them, it was more comfortable to talk to another baseball guy — namely, Hargrove.

Hargrove himself had trouble discussing it. What was he supposed to say? What words do you use when words seem not to matter? He slept little and cried more than he ever thought he could. As for trying to win baseball games, it was hard for him to concentrate. In the words of General Manager John Hart, "Mike was just out of it for the first half of that 1993 season. The accident ate him up."

Super Joe Charboneau's quick rise and fast fall is supposed to be a tragedy. So is the line drive that hit Herb Score in the eye, robbing him of greatness. So is the Indians' trade of Rocky Colavito in the spring of 1960. So is any one of the other major blunders that have haunted this franchise for nearly 40 years.

But the boating accident is what people in the real world mean when they talk about tragedy. It is when someone loses his life, or at least the life he once had.

Still, from a baseball standpoint, too, the boating accident was a tragedy.

Ojeda was a lefty who had won 113 big-league games when the Indians signed him before the 1993 season. Crews was an experienced right-hander expected to help in long relief. Then there was Olin, "a guy with the heart of a lion and the guts of a burglar to throw that fringe stuff up there and get people out," according to Hart.

Olin didn't throw hard. He didn't even throw normally. He was a submarine pitcher, delivering the ball to the plate from somewhere near his hip. Even while he was the top reliever in the farm system in the late 1980s, the Indians thought he was a gimmick guy who might be able to get a few right-handers out.

Instead, Olin became one of the better relief pitchers in the history of this franchise — at least for the last 18 months of his life. In 1991 Olin didn't save his first game until after the All-Star break, and then he went on to finish with 17 saves for the year. The next season, he saved 29 more games — that gave him 46 saves in a year and a half. Or, look at it this way: Olin saved 46 of the 104 games the Indians won in that same time span.

From a pure baseball standpoint, that is what Olin meant to this franchise in the spring of 1993. He was only 27. For Hargrove, he was the ultimate security blanket. If Hargrove had a lead late in the game, he knew he could hand the ball to Olin and not worry.

Olin's death was a horrendous loss to his family. The Indians felt a similar pain because he was one of their most popular players, a rock of a guy who had convinced teammate Kevin Wickander to go into a rehabilitation center and attack his drinking problem. Olin was a patient man with a dry sense of humor; he was the kind of reliable person you wanted to watch your house and children when you had to go out of town for the weekend. He was long and lean, all arms and legs that made him seem taller than his 6-foot-2 frame. If one Tribe player in the spring of 1993 could have been cast as a young Jimmy Stewart, it would have been Olin.

That is why Hargrove took Olin's death as if he had lost a younger brother. Hargrove had managed Olin in the minors. He and pitching coach Rick Adair had nurtured Olin and stuck by him when others in the Tribe organization had major doubts about Olin's major league future. Hargrove liked Olin as a player, as a person, and for how he bucked the odds.

Hargrove had been with the Indians organization for 11 seasons by the spring of 1993. This was supposed to be a year of hope, the final year at Cleveland Stadium, with the promise of a young team growing into a new park. The Indians were 76-86 in 1992, why couldn't they be at least a .500 team in 1993? Maybe they could even turn that 76-86 record around.

Instead, 1993 was the season of tears, and Hargrove began to ask himself, "What next?"

Or, as his wife Sharon recalled, "Mike would come home and say that things couldn't get any worse — then something would happen and it would get worse."

As the Indians staggered through the 1993 season with another 76-86 record, there was no way to begin to guess that this same team would win more games than any other in baseball just two years later — and that is why it is worth remembering what 1993 was like for the team and its fans.

The 1993 season became one of bittersweet memories for Indians fans.

The Wreck on the Lake known as Cleveland Stadium was a great place for spiderwebs and poles. The Indians played their first full game there on July 31, 1932. Naturally, they lost as Philadelphia's Lefty Grove beat Mel Harder, 1-0. The Indians divided their games between old League Park on Cleveland's east side and the Stadium until 1947, when the Indians moved to the lakefront full-time.

How you feel about the Stadium probably depends upon when you discovered baseball. For those who remember 1948, when Bill Veeck owned the team and turned the place into a party of 80,000 fans who watched the Indians win the pennant and the World Series, there will never be a better place to be than Cleveland Stadium in 1948. They will tell you about Lou Boudreau, the boy-manager . . . and they will talk of Lemon-Feller-Garcia-and-Wynn, those four pitchers always mentioned together as if they were joined at the hips. They will tell you about guys named Satchel Paige and Gene Bearden. They will tell you about a team that had to win a one-game playoff just to make the World Series — and did, beating Boston in Fenway Park. Then they will talk about another team from Boston, this one called the Boston Braves, and about how the Indians beat them in six games to win the World Series — their last World Series.

Those who came to baseball in the 1950s will remember a good team, but one frustrated by being sentenced to the same league as the New York Yankees. That is when Beacon Journal veteran baseball writer Sheldon Ocker found the Tribe. He once wrote: "In those days, nobody complained that the Stadium was too big or that the clubhouses were too small, the playing field was unkempt, that the scoreboard was three generations of technology behind, that the concrete was brittle, that the plumbing was archaic . . . and that the wind and the insects and the damp cold were reasons to stay away. Nobody ever heard of luxury suites in the 1950s. Fireworks were for the Fourth of July, not the ballpark. Fans never called talk shows to complain that the team had run out of free caps. In those days, the Indians didn't give anything away, and fans would never have thought to call a radio station."

Or, as the late Cleveland broadcaster Nev Chandler once told me, "The Stadium of my youth was a place where there were the old guys selling programs, where you walked in the gate and immediately smelled hot dogs on the grill and beer on tap. The crowds were big; the team was good. That was back in the 1950s. Herb Score was my favorite player. When I started doing the Indians games on radio with Herb Score in 1980, I used to wonder whatever happened to those days."

The Indians of the 1950s had the second-best record in the American League for the entire decade — behind the Yankees. And that was usually where they finished — right behind the Yankees. Al Lopez managed the team from 1951 to 1956. He finished in second place five times. The other year was 1954, when Lopez led the Indians to 111 victories, still the most ever by any major league team in a single season. But that great team was swept in four games by the New York Giants in the World Series.

The Indians came into my life in the early 1960s. By then, the team was bad and the crowds were small. The first baseball player I ever met was pitcher Jim "Mudcat" Grant. It was the last day of a Tribe season, sometime during the early 1960s. The game was over and my father and I were walking out of the park.

"That's Mudcat Grant," my father said, pointing to a tall man in a sharp, dark suit. He had a garment bag over one shoulder, a suitcase in his other hand. I was 8 years old and approached him slowly.

"How you doing, little man?" Grant said.

I was so astounded to be this close to a player, no words would come out of my tight throat. He saw that I had a scorecard and pen in my hand. He took them from me and signed his name. I whispered a thank-you.

"Any time, young fella, any time," he said, giving me a huge smile.

I've always thought Mudcat Grant was one of the best people I've ever met, and when I did run into him 20-some years later, he was still a nice, gracious man.

The next ballplayer I got to meet was Tribe pitcher Gary Bell. It's a long story, but I ended up in the same car as Bell. My older brother was driving, Bell was in the passenger seat, and I was sitting in the back. My brother told me not to ask any stupid questions.

I tried to take his advice. But I was 9 years old and I wanted to say *something*. So I came up with, "Who's the toughest hitter you've ever faced?"

My brother looked back over his shoulder, glaring at me. Of course, I ask the same kind of stupid questions now, only I get paid for doing it.

Anyway, Bell laughed and said, "The one with the bat."

Then Bell reached into his pocket, pulling out a pack of chewing tobacco. I don't remember anything else about that trip except that Bell was chewing tobacco and kept squirting juice out of the window. How would you like to have been driving behind us? Better hope your windows were closed and your wipers worked. As the ride progressed, it seemed to me that Bell spent more time hanging his head out of the window than a beagle trying to keep a good breeze on his nose.

I thought of all this during the last weekend of the 1993 season.

The Indians decided that no one could buy a ticket to just *one* game during the final weekend. You had to buy the three-game package or forget it. The Indians figured they would sell some 70,000 tickets for the final game, so why not have three 70,000-plus crowds? Knowing the Tribe fans' thirst for nostalgia — and having a hard enough hide to take the slings and arrows from fans who said the package deal was really a rip-off — the Indians said three games or no games, take it or leave it.

The fans took it, and the Indians averaged slightly over 72,000 for the three games and made more than $1 million for the weekend.

For those who bought the tickets, this weekend wasn't about making a quick buck.

For most, it was a time to remember Gary Bell, Jim Grant, Joe Charboneau or whichever player meant something to them. In the end, especially after seeing Jacobs Field, most Indians fans would admit that the Stadium was a dump, but it was "our" dump.

You could talk to any of those 72,000 fans, and each would tell you something different about what the Indians and the Stadium meant to him.

To me, it meant my father.

I thought of Tom Pluto on that last day of the 1993 season, and of how there are things we all wish we could do over. My father grew up on the east side of Cleveland and lived in the area until 1986, when he moved to Sarasota, Fla. He would come back to Cleveland every summer, visiting his sister and me.

"I'd like to see one more game at the Stadium," he told me sometime during the summer of 1993.

I said that sounded like fun, but we never got around to it. The truth was that I could have found a way to make it happen, but didn't — I was too busy, etc. The truth was that there were other things I considered more important than going to a ballgame with the man who took me to so many games when I was young. I see that now. Back then, it was one of those things that just didn't work out.

Anyway, my father returned to Florida in early September, and I went on with my life. But on Sept. 10, 1993 — a date I'll never forget — my father had a stroke. The man who first took me to an Indians game, the man who loved the Indians as if they were a part of his family, the man who had the most to do with my being a sportswriter — well, the stroke nearly killed him.

Now, this big, strapping guy can't move his right arm or his right leg. He can barely speak. His favorite word — and one he says constantly — is "man." He uses "man" to mean anything from being happy to being sad to having to go to the restroom. The irony is heavy. Both of his parents were Slovak, and little English was spoken in his home when he grew up. But he worked to learn the language, to embrace it as his own. Now, he can barely speak any language.

I thought about him as I sat in the press box for the Indians' last game at the Stadium. I thought about how we used to buy general admission tickets, then after a few innings, we'd sneak down into the box seats, usually about 20 rows up behind home plate. Our plan was to first stop at the concession stands, load up with popcorn and Cokes, then head straight to a couple of empty choice seats.

"Just follow me and look like you know what you are doing," he'd tell me, then grab my hand.

By the fourth inning, most ushers didn't care who sat where. They usually had 65,000 empty seats at the park.

That is something that kids from today will miss. With Jacobs Field and the Indians being chic, many kids and their dads can't even buy tickets to sit in the top row in the right-field corner. Forget moving down to the great seats; there are people in them and ushers guarding them like storm troopers to keep out the unwashed masses who can't afford a zillion bucks a year for season tickets.

When my father and I sat behind the plate, he'd talk baseball — how the count on the batter often dictated what happened, how a runner was getting a good lead off first base, how an outfielder was throwing to the wrong base. He wasn't a blowhard know-it-all or a manager-basher; he was just a guy who knew baseball and wanted to tell his son about the game.

Those were lessons that I never forgot, lessons that served me well during the six years when covering big-league baseball was my only job. I tried to remember his philosophy of living with the Indians all those years: "They may not have good teams, but they can still have some good players. You should respect that."

My father did because he spent a summer in the low minors right before World War II. Unlike a lot of guys who played a little pro ball before the war, he never said that the Army cost him a big-league career.

"I couldn't hit," he said. "I had a big-league glove at first base, but I couldn't hit. I played on Army teams with a lot of big-leaguers. I could see how much better they were than me."

What I didn't find out until years later — and it came from one of his old Army buddies — was that my father was respected enough to have actually managed an Army team that had five former big-leaguers on its roster.

Since his stroke, baseball has been one of the things that has helped us. His speech has been stolen from him, and that makes conversation a chore — sometimes nothing short of agony. But we can usually kill time by my telling him about the Indians of today. I remember how excited he was to hear about the big crowds during that last weekend in 1993 and then about the new ballpark. I told him that I'd buy him tickets to Jacobs Field, but as I said that, I was pretty sure it would never happen.

He knew it, too. He sat in his wheelchair. He was 73 before his stroke and looked about 60. Now, he was smaller, a little withered, with slumped shoulders and deep-set, sad eyes. He looked at least 80.

I told him that 1993 was a rough year. I reminded him about how the Indians had lost Tim Crews and Steve Olin and about how we had gone through his stroke. I said that 1994 had to be better — as Mike Hargrove used to ask, "How can it get any worse?" But my father was afraid to hear the answer to that question.

My father shrugged. He began to cry. In the past, this would have really upset me because he seldom cried. But stroke victims with speech problems cry a lot — when they are happy, when they are upset, or when they are frustrated because the words won't come.

So he cried and I hugged him. There was nothing else to do, nothing to be said. Some people will tell you that their lives changed when the Indians moved from Cleveland Stadium to Jacobs Field. I know exactly what they mean.

3

GETTING TO KNOW YOU

The Indians couldn't wait to get to 1994. The deaths of Steve Olin and Tim Crews were behind them. Bobby Ojeda decided not to remain with the team. "Too many ghosts," he explained.

The Stadium was gone. For all the goo and nostalgia in the final weekend of 1993, the fact was that the Tribe lost all three games at the Stadium — a fitting send-off. They finished with a 76-86 record in 1993, an exact repeat of their 1992 mark.

Well, 1994 was supposed to be different.

With Jacobs Field ensuring close to two million tickets sold, General Manager John Hart was able to convince owner Dick Jacobs to play the heavy in the free-agent game. The days of Scott Scudder, Jack Armstrong and Jesse Orosco were over — it was time to get some real players.

Hart wanted a big-time starter to anchor the rotation and a big hitter to bat behind Albert Belle. These had to be proven, experienced guys. They also had to be players who would not demand long-term contracts. Hart went free-agent shopping with the idea of signing a player, not marrying him and agreeing to pay for his funeral.

Two-year deals would be tops.

For four years, Hart and Indians President Hank Peters had been preaching patience. They had been saying that the payroll was being cut not because Dick Jacobs was cheap, but because the money was going into the farm system to build for the future. It was a five-year plan.

Right, said the fans. Right, said the media. A five-year plan. For the last 30 years, the Indians have had five-year plans — and they changed them every two years.

"We will sign quality free agents when we are ready to compete," Hart had said.

In 1994, Hart said it was time, although few fans took him seriously. Yes, they liked a lot of the Tribe's young players, but deep in their hearts most fans expected something to go wrong. They couldn't help it. Every Indians fan had a part of his heart that was like the dark side of the moon. Even Hart himself occasionally had to battle the blues.

"I remember those winters in the early 1990s when we'd be on our press caravan, going from town to town in about five feet of snow," he said. "I'd stand up there and try to sell a team that had Jose Escobar. I mean, there were times when I felt I should put a big speaker on top of my car and drive around, talking about the Indians to anyone who would listen. I was willing to do anything to sell a few tickets, but not a lot of people were buying."

Hart had hoped that would change in 1993. He thought a .500 record was possible — maybe even contention if everything fell into place. And if the team started fast, he thought he could convince Dick Jacobs to make a few midseason deals for high-priced veterans to help in a pennant push.

But the deaths of Olin and Crews killed the season and put those plans on hold for another year.

With the team moving into Jacobs Field for 1994, Hart wanted to do something dramatic. Yes, the team was selling tickets at a faster pace than at any time since the 1950s, but he also knew that the fans paying the higher prices at Jacobs Field would want more for their money.

With a starting rotation of Charles Nagy (coming off shoulder surgery), Jose Mesa and a bunch of kids, Hart knew there was trouble. Yes, the team also needed a stopper in the bullpen, but there would be few leads to protect.

You can write down this date: Dec. 2, 1993. That was the day when Indians fans learned that Hart and Jacobs were different from the general managers and owners who had come before them. On Dec. 2, 1993, Hart announced the signings of Dennis Martinez and Eddie Murray.

A few fans saw both players bearing down on 40 and said, "It's Wayne Garland and Keith Hernandez all over again."

Baseball people knew better.

Martinez was 15-9 with a 3.85 ERA in 1993 for Montreal. Ever since beating his alcohol problems and dropping into the minors in 1987, Martinez had been a physical fitness fanatic. He avoided major injuries. If he was hurting, he pitched through it. As Hart said, "Not only did Dennis win a lot of games in Montreal, but he pitched a lot of innings."

Hart looked at the fact that from 1989 to 1993, Martinez averaged more than seven innings a start. He was one of only seven pitchers in baseball history to win at least 100 games in each league. Hart knew that Martinez had a 55-4 record when he was backed with at least four runs, and Hart was sure the Indians would score, and score a lot, in 1994.

It was a no-brainer.

Martinez lived in Miami. Hart flew him to Cleveland and spent the day with the right-hander, showing him the downtown renaissance and the plush suburbs. He took him to a couple of terrific restaurants. Then he showed him Jacobs Field.

Martinez could not believe how the city had changed since his last trip to Cleveland. That was in 1985 as a member of the Baltimore Orioles. He loved the new ballpark, but looked at the cozy left-field wall and said, "That's kind of close, isn't it?"

"Dennis, don't worry," Hart said. "The wind *always blows in* from left field, right into the batter's face."

Martinez was sold, especially when he heard the Indians were willing to pay him close to $9 million for two years.

He was 38 years old. He knew a good deal when he heard one. He signed without even bothering to check with the other teams who had expressed an interest in him.

Hart was also talking to Murray, who didn't need a trip to Cleveland. He had heard good things from his baseball friends about Dick Jacobs, Hart and the Indians. He had just spent two miserable years with the Mets, and wanted out of the media fishbowl that is New York. Murray was looking for a smaller city where he could be left alone and just play ball.

Hart said that was Cleveland.

He told Murray that the Indians really didn't need a first baseman; he could be the designated hitter. Being a DH would lengthen Murray's career, saving his legs. Murray liked that because he had been bothered by a variety of muscle pulls. He was once a Gold Glove first baseman, but he knew his skills had eroded. What he still did best was swing the bat, and the idea of only having to swing the bat was intriguing.

Murray then asked about the ballpark.

"Eddie, you'll love it," Hart said. "The wind *always blows out*!"

Hart then put a two-year, $6 million offer in front of Murray.

The deal was done.

Hart later snagged another big-name free agent in pitcher Jack Morris, who was at the end of his career and signed for $500,000. Hart figured if Morris worked out, great. If not, they'd cut him and it wouldn't cost much.

Suddenly, the Indians were playing baseball like the big boys.

When the 1994 season opened, Mike Hargrove was on the spot.

Hart and Hargrove had come together as a shotgun marriage arranged by former team president Hank Peters.

It was Peters who hired Hart away from the Orioles in 1989, taking a third-base coach who had never worked in the front office before and making him an assistant general manager. At that time Peters knew that he would retire within two years. He thought Hart would be the best man to take over the team — even though Hart had no experience in that area before. But Peters loved Hart's relentless drive and his intelligence.

In the end, it came down to a gut feeling, and Peters' instinct told him that Hart would be the man who would continue the work he had begun with the Tribe.

While he trained Hart, Peters also was developing Hargrove to manage the team. An Indians first baseman from 1979 to 1985, Hargrove had worked at every level of the Tribe's farm system, beginning as a batting coach at Class A Batavia in 1986 and winding up as the Class AAA Pacific Coast League Manager of the Year at Colorado Springs in 1989. In 1990, Peters was in the market for a new manager. He interviewed Hargrove, but hired an old friend, John McNamara.

But Peters told McNamara: "Mike is going to be on your coaching staff. Eventually, he is going to be a big-league manager. I want you to teach him everything he needs to know."

For the next year and a half, McNamara trained the man he knew would take his job. Long after games, they'd sit in McNamara's office and he'd say, "Mike, when you are managing this team, here is what you should think about . . . "

One of Peters' final moves was firing McNamara during the 1991 All-Star break and replacing him with Hargrove. Then at the end of the 1991 season, Peters retired and Hart moved up.

That's how Hargrove and Hart came together.

But in Hart's first two years as general manager, Hargrove had 76-86 records. The two men didn't know each other well. There also was a certain uneasiness that came from their unique situation. No baseball executive had ever groomed a general manager and a manager in the manner that Peters had done with Hart and Hargrove. Most executives are far too worried about covering their own butts and convincing the owners to give them a few more years on a contract; the last thing they want to do is bring in men who can take their places.

But Hank Peters always was an honest, conservative man of little ego whose agenda was up front. He had come to Cleveland in 1987 knowing it was his last stop, and he had promised Dick Jacobs that he'd leave when the franchise was on its own two feet and ready to make the great leap forward. He also had told Jacobs that he'd put the team in the hands of men he trusted.

Understand this much about the relationship between Dick Jacobs and Hank Peters: If Hank Peters told Jacobs that Lake Erie was about to dry up, Jacobs would begin buying the land now under water as prospective sites for new shopping malls. He had complete faith in the integrity of Peters.

So Hart and Hargrove moved up courtesy of Peters, who then departed.

"It is true that Hank wanted to change managers during the (1991) All-Star break," Hart said. "But I signed off on the decision to promote Mike. Hank was retiring at the end of the season, and he was not about to stick me with a manager whom I didn't want."

Or as Hargrove said, "I never thought I was shoved down John's throat."

But it did take a while for these two men to develop an appetite for each other.

Usually, a general manager likes to hire his own manager. Sometimes, it is a friend. Other times, it is a hired gun with a history of quick fixes a Billy Martin or a Dick Williams. But no matter who the manager is, the general manager feels better if his handpicked choice is in the dugout.

On the other hand, the manager likes to know that the general manager loves him. The GM puts his reputation on the line when he hires a manager, so the GM won't be too quick to make the manager the sacrificial lamb during the first major losing streak. At least a manager hopes that's the case.

But Hart and Hargrove didn't have those ties to each other. They also have two very different personalities.

"I didn't know how much confidence John Hart had in me," Hargrove said. "Really, I didn't know John that well at all."

And when they did spend time with each other, they each had their doubts.

"John is a guy in perpetual motion," Hargrove said. "With him, everything is go, go, go! It's do, do, do! His concentration is on the team 20 hours a day. He sleeps only four, and even in his down time he's thinking about the team."

Hargrove is from Perryton, Texas, where folks talk slowly and are careful of what they say. They believe that there is a place for work and a place for family and that there is nothing wrong with a good night's sleep.

"If I tried to keep John's pace, I would just get overloaded," Hargrove said. "I mean, I usually work 12 to 14 hours a day, but I also like to get away from baseball at least for a few hours a day. If I don't, I'm not as productive."

Hart would come to Hargrove with a dozen different ideas — trades, minor league call-ups, players shifting positions. He didn't mean for Hargrove to try them all, or even most of them.

But Hargrove thought Hart was serious about everything.

Hart is like Billy the Kid, who would pull out two six-guns and almost blindly blast at a target hoping one shot would hit. Hargrove is a hunter, and he knows that you often only get one shot, so you better make it a good one.

"At first, Mike didn't know how to read me," Hart said. "I asked him to be organized at all times, to write things down and make plans. I didn't tell him what to do in terms of making out a lineup and things like that, but I wanted to know what he planned to do and why he wanted to do it.

"Also, I like spirited debates. Sometimes, I throw out an idea just to get a response, to generate others' ideas that might be better. The conversations can get a little confrontational, and I don't think Mike was used to that, either."

Hargrove believed that he had to keep talking Hart out of making moves, and Hart was convinced that he had to push Hargrove to be more daring, to take more chances.

Hargrove was thinking, "Hart needs to chill out and look at the big picture." Hart believed, "Hargrove needs a kick in the butt."

"That was exactly how it was between us the first two years," Hargrove said. "We both had to get over some hurdles so we could come to an understanding. He needed to see that I was just as intense — in my own way — as he is. And I needed to feel confident to say, 'John, that's really not a good idea.' "

Hart was a minor league manager for six years, and all of his teams made the playoffs and had winning records. He was the 1986 Minor

League Manager of the Year at Class AAA Rochester in the Baltimore farm system.

"I was on the fast track to become a big-league manager when Hank Peters hired me as his assistant," Hart said. "It was a tough decision for me to give up being on the field and move into the front office."

Peters said that was why he made Hart the interim manager at the end of the 1989 season after Doc Edwards was fired. The team had an 8-11 record under Hart.

"I wanted John to get managing out of his system, so I let him have a taste of it," Peters said. "But I also told John that it was temporary. Get a good look at the players, then come back upstairs and help me turn this thing around."

Said Hart: "I could manage in the big leagues if I had to, but I've found this job to be so big that I don't have any ambition to be in the dugout."

But in 1992 and 1993, Hargrove wasn't so sure of that. He took Hart's suggestions and criticism as second-guessing, as if Hart were saying, "I could do this better."

The flash point between the two came in the spring of 1993.

"We had a meeting where John gave me a job evaluation," Hargrove said. "John talked about my good qualities, and there were a lot of nice things he said. But I didn't hear a word. All I heard him say was, 'You *don't* do this, you *don't* do that.' It got heated, and I thought it was pretty unfair. He told me what he thought of me as a manager, and I told him about some of things he did that annoyed and frustrated me. We put our cards on the table."

Hart wanted Hargrove to be more aggressive, in terms of running a game and in the clubhouse. He also wanted more things written down.

"I told Mike that he could be a good manager for a long time," Hart said. "Then I told him what he had to do to become that kind of manag er. He strongly disagreed with some of the things I had to say. But to his credit, he began addressing those questions in his own way."

Not long after that meeting in 1993, Tribe pitchers Steve Olin and Tim Crews were killed in a boating accident. The Indians went into a state of shock, and Hargrove found himself being more of a grief counselor than a manager. At midseason, the Indians were in last place.

"There were a couple of times in 1993 when I thought I might be fired," Hargrove said. "There were times when I wondered if we were pulling in the same direction."

But Hart stayed with Hargrove and the team finished with a 76-86 record in 1993. Hargrove's contract was up at the end of 1994, and when that season began, Hart was mum on the subject of an extension.

"I knew that Mike was good with a young club," Hart said. "I wanted to see what he'd do with a contender."

As the 1994 season began, Hargrove wasn't thrilled about having only one year left on his contract. It would be easy for some players to decide that he was a lame duck. Why not? Most of the team had three-to-five-year deals, why not the manager?

Hargrove also thought that Hart had taken his time in extending his contract back in 1992. And while the deal did carry through 1994 — so that was some security — Hargrove was one of the lowest-paid managers in the big leagues at $225,000.

Hart, meanwhile, was still trying to size up Hargrove. He knew that Hargrove was a steady, decent man with endless compassion; he had demonstrated that during the boating accident in 1993. He also realized that Hargrove had the respect of his players and that he also had the patience to develop a young team.

But did Hargrove have the drive to push a team to its limit? Could he take 25 guys and convince them to capture the hill, plant the flag, and do it right in the face of enemy fire? It was going to take a special man to be the first Indians manager to win a title since Al Lopez in 1954, and Hart had no way of knowing if Hargrove would be the guy.

So Hargrove opened the 1994 season knowing that his job was on the line. On the other hand, Hart's job was secure. Dick Jacobs was convinced that Hart's energy and vision were exactly what the Indians needed.

In the end, the decision on Hargrove would be made by Hart.

Hart said that 1994 "would be a breakthrough year." He didn't predict a pennant, but insisted that the team was a contender. If they didn't beat out the Chicago White Sox for the new Central Division title, they certainly should be one of the teams competing for a wild card spot in the playoffs.

Hargrove thought that Hart was correct — as long as the team stayed healthy and everything went right. But these were the Indians. Hargrove had played, coached and managed in Cleveland for 11 years. Since when did everyone stay healthy and everything follow the plan?

He would have liked a contract extension at the start of the year, but he heard nothing from Hart. And Hart was very evasive when discussing Hargrove's future with the media. He certainly didn't bury his manager. Nor did he give Hargrove a phony vote of confidence. He simply said little and did it in his usual stream-of-consciousness style, consuming about a million words a minute.

Hart also had fired Rick Adair, the 1993 pitching coach and a friend of Hargrove's. Hart didn't demand that Hargrove hire Phil Regan as a replacement, but he suggested it. Hargrove interviewed Regan and liked him. Also, Hargrove knew it wasn't smart to buck Hart on this issue — especially since Regan was qualified and seemed like a decent human being.

Regan had spent the previous six years as a major league scout for the Dodgers. He also had been a pitching coach in Seattle and had been a big-league pitcher for 13 years. But Regan's real goal was to manage, and he had been a manager in various Latin American winter leagues for 10 years.

Hart also thought Regan was built from managerial timber. Did this mean he wanted to hire Regan with the idea of him replacing Hargrove? Not necessarily. But having Regan close meant that Hart did have an option if the 1994 season turned sour.

As the Indians entered June, their record was only 26-21. Hart still gave no public hint about Hargrove's future. In fact, he worried Hargrove when he told the Beacon Journal that the team's start was "about average." He also was concerned about some of the blunders on defense and the bullpen. He gave Hargrove support, but refused to discuss the contract extension.

None of this thrilled Hargrove.

Then the Indians were 18-9 in the month of June. With Martinez, Morris, Mark Clark and Charles Nagy molding together to form a reliable starting rotation, the Indians indeed had become a contender.

Hargrove had always been popular with the media because he played it straight with them. If he couldn't answer a question, he'd just say that he couldn't discuss it right now. Otherwise, he was candid and insightful. So the scribes and talk show hosts began putting the heat on Hart to rehire Hargrove. What was he waiting for?

In July, Hart did just that, signing Hargrove for the 1995, 1996 and 1997 seasons.

The Tribe continued to play well. Regan demonstrated that he was an excellent pitching coach and loyal to Hargrove. He also was the man who first suggested putting Jose Mesa in the bullpen, although that would not pan out until 1995. After the 1994 season, Regan was so highly regarded that Baltimore hired him as its manager. Then Hargrove and Hart named Mark Wiley as the pitching coach. Wiley had been the Tribe's pitching coach from 1988 to 1991; then he was a scout for the team. The Indians knew and respected Wiley, and he helped fashion a staff that had the lowest ERA in the American League in 1995. The Indians had depth, even in the coaching ranks.

The Indians stayed close to the White Sox in July and early August of 1994. For the first time since 1959, the Tribe was headed for a pennant race. The year was everything Hart had envisioned, and he knew that Hargrove helped bring it together. For his part, Hargrove appreciated how Hart aggressively signed Martinez, Murray and other free agents.

Hart has made a study of general manager-manager relationships.

"I've seen GMs who took a total hands-off approach, and they had their managers and clubs run away from them," Hart said. "I decided that I'd be hands-on. I don't meddle. But in spring training, I have a say in who makes the club. I'll listen to input from the staff, but in the end, I'll make the deals."

For example, it was Hart's idea to promote Manny Ramirez, a raw rookie outfielder, at the start of the 1994 season.

"I've never told Mike who to play," Hart said. "Most of the time, I'm flexible. But there are some moments when a general manager must say, 'This is how it's going to be.' "

Hargrove said, "I've learned that when John says, 'Mike, for what it's worth . . . ' — well, I better pay close attention. John McNamara used to tell me, 'It's imperative that you have a good relationship with your GM,' and he was right. It's like a marriage. You both want the same things, but you have different ways to get there — and sometimes, you are going to clash.

"I now think that John (Hart) is the best GM in baseball, and I've heard him say that I'm the best manager. We still have a boss-employee relationship, but there are things I can say to John as a friend that I don't think a lot of managers can tell their GMs. Sometimes, he says something to me that, if it came from someone else, I'd tell the guy to go sit in a chair in the corner of the room, and I'd go on down the road. John and I have grown together in our jobs and learned from each other, and I don't know how often that happens in this business."

As Hart and Hargrove came to an appreciation of each other during the 1994 season, Jacobs Field was indeed a field of dreams for the team and the fans. This was to be a September to remember.

Only there would be no September baseball in Cleveland in 1994.

4

SUMMER VACATION

If fans had been in the dressing room on the day the Tribe players walked out, they never would have bought a ticket to another game.

It was the afternoon of Aug. 10, 1994.

Aug. 10 also happens to be the birthday of Rocky Colavito. I'm not saying that he cursed the team. In fact, it was Colavito who told me: "I keep getting letters from Cleveland fans who say that it seems like the team has been cursed ever since they traded me."

He meant the first trade, the one to Detroit for Harvey Kuenn in the spring of 1960. Colavito led the American League with 42 homers (along with Minnesota's Harmon Killebrew) in 1959. That was the last time any member of the Indians led the league in homers, and 1959 was the last time the Indians were in a pennant race — at least until Aug. 10, 1994.

The Curse of Rocky Colavito was hatched on the day General Manager Frank Lane traded him to the Detroit Tigers. It continued in 1965, when General Manager Gabe Paul made an even worse deal to bring him back — giving up the Tribe's two best prospects for the 31-year-old Colavito.

The first prospect was lefty Tommy John. In 1964, John was only 2-9 for the Tribe. "Tommy was a great guy on a ballclub, but he didn't throw that hard and I didn't know if he was tough enough to be a great pitcher," Paul said. "I guess I was wrong."

John was only a .500 pitcher with the White Sox, until he blew out his elbow in 1972. Then he had radical surgery, which consisted of transplanting a tendon from his leg into his left elbow, and he came back as a Hall of Fame-caliber pitcher. The surgery is now known as "The Tommy John Operation" in baseball circles, and it is employed often — although seldom with the same dramatic results.

Tribe fans looked at John's injury and his startling comeback and thought: "If he had stayed with the Indians and had that operation, the doctor probably would have accidentally cut off his arm!"

Anyway, Tommy John won 286 games after the Tribe traded him.

The second prospect traded for Colavito was outfielder Tommie Agee, who went on to play for nine years and was a World Series hero with the Mets in 1969.

The Indians also gave up a third player in the deal, a serviceable catcher named John Romano. He was supposed to have been the key guy when the trade was announced, but he ended up being the least significant.

As for Colavito, he led the American League with 108 RBI in 1965. He also hit .287 with 26 homers and played all 162 games in right field without committing an error. The 1965 Indians had a fine 87-75 record — their best since 1959 — but that was only good for fifth place, 15 games back.

In 1966, Colavito hit 30 homers, but batted only .238. Age was catching up with him, and on June 30, 1967, Colavito was traded to the White Sox for Jimmy King, an obscure 34-year-old outfielder with a .240 batting average. More importantly, the Indians received $50,000 in the deal, helping Gabe Paul meet the July 1967 payroll. Colavito played sparingly and retired after the 1968 season with a lifetime record of 374 homers and a .266 batting average.

Well, on Rocky Colavito's 61st birthday, the Indians beat the Blue Jays, 5-3, at the Skydome. Jason Grimsley was the winning pitcher, which tells you that it wasn't just another day at the ballpark, because it isn't often that Grimsley wins in the major leagues. Even Omar Vizquel made an error, which also tells you something.

During the game, the contract talks between Players Association chief Donald Fehr and the owners' negotiator Richard Ravitch broke off. No new talks were scheduled. The union had said it would strike on Aug. 12 unless a contract was reached. Since the Indians had no game on Aug. 11, as they walked out of the Skydome on Aug. 10, they knew a strike was certain.

Guess what.

Most of them didn't care. They seemed almost giddy, like kids on the last day of school.

The Indians were only a game behind the first-place White Sox. They were in position to be the wild card team in the new playoff format. Would they have liked to finish the season? Sure. Were they heartbroken? Guess again.

They had been thinking about Aug. 12, 1994, for over a month. That's how long the strike date had been set, and most players assumed there would indeed be a strike. Not just the Indians, but major league players everywhere were like rich college kids planning their spring breaks.

Pitchers Eric Plunk and Derek Lilliquist had arranged a deep-sea fishing trip to Cabo San Lucas, Mexico. Paul Sorrento had recently moved to Florida and talked about checking out that state's fine golf courses. Dennis Martinez seemed to set the tone when he said, "Players' wives and kids have been making big plans for what they'll do the next few weeks during the strike. If those plans get canceled (because of a strike settlement), I know that some families won't be happy. My wife and kids keep telling me, 'We hope you're home the next few weeks so you can play with us.' That is what many people are thinking."

Do you believe these guys?

It is hard for most of us to comprehend what it means to be a millionaire 10 times over. If they missed a couple of checks — even if those checks were worth more than what most people earn in a year — well, the players weren't worried. To them, it was worth it to have a few weeks off.

That is how they looked at a strike — a two-week vacation. They'd be back sometime in September to finish the regular season and then begin the playoffs. A couple of players even suggested that the union push for a two-week break in the middle of every season, so the players and their families could take a summer vacation. You were tempted to believe they were just kidding around, but it was hard to be sure.

John Hart and Mike Hargrove were depressed. So was Tony Pena, the veteran catcher who knew that the clock was running down on his career. Eddie Murray and Martinez had been through so many strikes, they thought of strikes like the weather — there was nothing much they could do about it.

Hart went on and on about how a terrible thing was being done to the Cleveland fans. He talked about the damage that would be done to the game, especially if play didn't resume in time for a World Series. He seemed to be one of the few baseball people who really understood the serious consequences of the Aug. 12 strike.

Hargrove just sat behind his desk in the manager's office, looking glum and barely able to answer any question with more than a few soft words. The guy from the Texas Panhandle was so upset that he seemed ready to bite a hole through his lower lip. A season like 1994 was why Hargrove had decided to manage — and why he especially wanted to manage the Indians. He had seen nothing but darkness in his days with the Tribe, and now that the sun had finally peeked through the clouds, it had turned out to be nothing but a prelude to a thunderstorm.

All of this reminded me of something former Indians and sports philosopher Cory Snyder once said: "You know, baseball would be better off if they didn't let the fans into the games."

When the strike came, baseball did just that.

On Aug. 12, 1994, I went to Jacobs Field a few hours after baseball officially was on strike. At 3 in the afternoon, huge padlocks were on all the gates, but that didn't stop at least 20 fans from sticking their heads through the bars.

They were staring at the vacant baseball field. No one was playing. No one was going to play until Who Knew When.

"I just like looking at a baseball field, even if it's empty," one middle-aged fan told me. The Indians had been scheduled to play Milwaukee that night at Jacobs Field. Dennis Martinez was supposed to pitch. The fan said he didn't have tickets for the game (it was sold out), but he was in the neighborhood and wanted to stop by and see the field.

I ran into a couple of guys named John Cheblo and Ken Peters. They were looking through the bars in left field, pointing to a spot way back in the upper deck behind home plate.

"Those would have been our seats for tonight," Cheblo said.

Peters said he was from Cleveland, but now lived in Chicago. He'd planned a special trip to see friends and attend his first game at Jacobs Field. He was so excited about the Indians in a pennant race, but now there was no pennant race.

Some fans took pictures of each other in front of the Bob Feller statue and even by the ticket windows that were closed, with curtains drawn ominously down. One ticket window had a sign reading: "Tonight's game sold out." Next to it was a sign about strike refunds.

The baseball strike was being smothered by the media, with reporters trying to cover every conceivable angle. One Cleveland television station even did a tear-jerk report (OK, it was really a jerky report) on how the strike affected panhandlers around Jacobs Field. Hey, those guys with their styrofoam cups were going to take a beating, ya know. And it was all 'cause of dem spoiled ballplayers! One guy said it would cost him $50 a game.

Remember, this guy was begging, not working.

But is that so different from catcher Sandy Alomar saying that the players had to strike, "because some guys don't make a lot of money. Some aren't even making $500,000."

Hello?

The scary thing is that Alomar is one of the good guys. He was genuinely upset when the strike came, and he hadn't planned a vacation to Yellowstone or Cancun. He loves baseball and was so excited that he was finally healthy to play. It tore him up to follow the union out the clubhouse door.

Then he tried to be a good soldier, gave his views on the labor situation, and firmly planted both spiked shoes right down his throat.

I thought about Alomar and the nitwit panhandler story as I wandered over to the vendors' windows, where I met Nichola Woodward. She was a high school student from East Cleveland who worked at the concession stands for $6.25 an hour.

Most nights, she made $40 or $50, depending upon the length of the game. She had a check in her hand, her last paycheck of the summer. She also had a sheet in her hand telling her to return her concessionaire uniform in a week or pay $50 to keep it. Nichola Woodward didn't want the uniform. Nor did she expect a handout. She wanted more games and more hours so she could keep working and help her family.

The strike, "I don't get it," she said.

Some people were in the Indians gift shop. Two clerks agreed that business wasn't much worse than on any other day. People loved the Indians — especially these Indians who finally were winning — and they wanted souvenirs. They wanted to look at the field. They wanted to sit in the stands, or work at the concession stands.

The players would never understand any of it.

I realized that when Dennis Martinez compared the striking ballplayers to the Cuban boat people.

Like Alomar, Martinez is one of the good guys; he does love the game. But when most ballplayers talked about the strike, they came across like blooming idiots.

So there we were, in August of 1994. The Indians were in a pennant race, but there was no pennant race.

Baseball said it was on strike. The players said they were on vacation.

The fans — all they could do was look through the bars at an empty Jacobs Field.

5

Call Them Irreplaceable

When baseball owners and players pulled the plug on the 1994 World Series, Indians fans were angry. This was the team's first pennant race since 1959 and its first chance to win anything since 1954. History weighed heavily on everyone's mind.

John Hart held a press conference the day baseball went dark. He was nearly in tears. He was tasting a pennant drive, just like his team's fans.

"All we've wanted to do since we started building this team in 1989 is to do what we've done this year," he said. "It hurts — especially the fans. And I think there is a little Indians fan in everyone in America."

Some fans chalked it up to The Curse of Rocky Colavito, or whatever label they used to characterize the malaise that had hung over the franchise since the 1950s. Fans talked about Tony Horton's mental breakdown, the rise and incredibly quick fall of Super Joe Charboneau, Sam McDowell's drinking, Herb Score's eye injury, the deaths of Steve Olin and Tim Crews. The woeful litany seemed endless.

But the strike was different.

Those other things were calamities and tragedies. The strike was a stupidity.

"If ever there was a team that never should have gone on strike, it was the Indians," Hart said.

He talked about "nurturing the young players." He talked about the commitment the Indians had made to the players in the form of long-term contracts and about the decision by the core group of young players to stay together and see if they could win big in Cleveland. While the rest of baseball was involved in a guerrilla war, the owners and players in Cleveland were actually playing the same game.

And then there were no more games to be played.

The 1994 season officially died on Sept. 14. Like a lot of fans, I had heard enough. If the bums didn't want to play — fine; I'd find something else to do. There were always more books to read and movies to watch.

Then I went to visit my father in Florida. Tom Pluto is 75 years old and his love of sports is one of the main reasons that I became a sportswriter.

He also is a stroke victim, one of 1.3 million Americans afflicted every year.

Imagine a computer that short-circuits; that's what happens to the brain during a stroke. The damage usually is permanent, and the results can be quite bizarre.

My father loves to read, but now he can only read nouns — and not all nouns.

He was never much of a writer, but now he can't write at all. He's a right-hander, and the stroke paralyzed that side of his body. His right arm just hangs there, forgotten and useless. The only thing he feels in that arm is occasional sharp pain.

He can print with his left hand, but all he can print is his name and mine. He doesn't know what the letters mean. He just practiced a million times and memorized how to do the names so he can sign papers that he can't read.

My father loved to talk to me on the phone, especially to talk sports. Now he can barely talk at all. He mostly says one word — "man." And he must say, "Man . . . *man* . . . *MAN!*" a million times a day. How he says that word and where he points often tells you what he wants, but it doesn't do much for phone conversations or conversations with strangers.

He used to love to go out to eat, but now we have to be sure to stay near a bathroom. The stroke played havoc with his bladder and kidneys, and he constantly feels as if he has to go. This is a guy who can't use his right arm or leg, so going to the bathroom is about as easy as climbing a mountain of loose gravel. Where do I put my good arm? My paralyzed leg? Will I slip? Will I get there in time?

Then there is his right leg. After 18 months of therapy, he was able to move his paralyzed leg enough to cover about 25 steps in his walker — if the surface was flat and there was no traffic. But then he fell down, broke his right hip, and needed surgery to install a metal plate and six screws. He was bedridden for a month.

When I saw him after his hip operation, he told me that he missed baseball.

There are a lot of people like my father — retired, disabled, shut-in, forgotten. They spend much of what remains of their lives in front of a television set, and a lot of those folks are baseball fans.

My father was almost as angry at baseball as he was at the fates that sentenced him to life as a stroke victim. He couldn't understand why the games stopped. He would turn on ESPN and see tractor pulls, bowling and beach volleyball, but no baseball. When Players Association chief Donald Fehr or one of the owners would show up on the screen and try to explain the strike, my father would make a sour face and disgustedly wave his good hand at the TV.

I wished I could have gotten the players and owners together so I could have pushed my father's wheelchair into the room, allowing him to wave his left fist and scream, "Man . . . *man* . . . *MAN!*" at the men who had kidnapped his game. I wanted to see those bozos try to explain to him why they couldn't divide up a billion dollars and give him and all those like him some relief from their often boring and sad lives.

These are the people we forget about. They are the heart patients and the blind. They are people who have lost limbs and nearly lost their lives. Baseball isn't everything to them, but it is something and it is soothing. These folks often don't have much else.

During the strike, I didn't feel sorry for myself or for most Indians fans. We had other things to do; there were plenty of diversions available to the healthy.

But those involved in the baseball strike had a moral obligation to ask themselves why they sold out my father and all those others who needed the game the most.

When I thought about that, I got mad.

Now, I see that this was a dumb idea, but thinking about my father then was a reason that I supported replacement players in the spring of 1995. Somehow, someone had to start playing baseball again.

In the final weeks before spring training of 1995, John Hart was driving his staff to distraction.

He was the most frustrated man in baseball. He had put together this great team — the best Indians team since 1954 — yet he couldn't put it on the field. His lust for a pennant grew rabid. If he couldn't win with his regular guys, then he'd assemble the best replacement team in baseball.

"I figured that sooner or later, the regular players would come back," he said. "I thought about football during its strike and how the NFL played some replacement games and counted them in the standings. What if we had to play 20 games before the regulars got back? I knew we had a team good enough to get into the playoffs, but I didn't want our regular players to walk in the door and inherit a 2-18 record."

Hart and his key assistants, Dan O'Dowd and Mark Shapiro, made more than 700 calls to bring in players willing to cross the picket line.

"What were we supposed to do, keep the ballparks dark for another year?" Hart asked.

Hiring replacements appealed to Hart's nature. Not because he was a union buster, but because he believed in *doing something*, rather than sitting back and letting "Donald Fehr dictate the terms."

Fehr is the head of the Major League Players Association, and a case can be made that his union has been the toughest and most successful in the country over the last 20 years. The players are very loyal, and the union has been without scandal and has kept the players' interests at the forefront. Also, stupid and greedy owners forced the players to circle the wagons, especially in the 1970s when free agency was dawning but no one was sure what it meant or what impact it would have on the game.

But by the spring of 1995, the players had just as much power as the owners. The average salary was over $1 million, and they could shut down the game if the owners would not play ball when it came to a labor agreement.

Rather than wait out the impasse, Hart wanted to see some kind of baseball.

In the off-season, each major league team has a 40-man roster. Those players belonged to the union, and they were not about to cross the imaginary picket line. There were young players in the low minors not on the 40-man roster, but the union talked to them and said: "One day you will play in the big leagues, you will belong to the union and receive union benefits. You should support us now because we will take care of you later."

While some big-league players hinted of physical reprisals to those who broke ranks, most players didn't take the threats seriously. What made an impression was the thought of being shunned, of being labeled a scab and a strikebreaker.

The Major League Players Association has been through eight different strikes and has won huge concessions each time. Its members know how to be patient, how to close ranks, and how to make sure that they don't buckle under pressure.

So when Hart and other general managers went shopping for players, they were left with guys who were Has-Beens or Never-Weres.

They went shopping in places such as the Class A Northern League.

Its president is Miles Wolff, and the Northern League is sort of baseball's Last Chance Saloon. The franchises are in St. Paul, Minn.; Sioux Falls, S.D.; Sioux City, Iowa; Duluth, Minn.; Winnipeg, Manitoba, and Thunder Bay, Ontario.

None of these minor league teams are affiliated with the major leagues. They hire their own managers, sign their own players and play an 84-game schedule during the three summer months. That's partly because baseball was not meant to be played in the spring and fall along the shores of Gitche Gumee, as Lake Superior is known. Players earn about $4,000 for the summer, and their dream is to attract attention from a scout and be purchased by a major league team, which would allow them to continue their baseball careers in a fully sanctioned farm system.

"Most of our players had been in the minors for several years before they came to us," Wolff said. "A few were in the big leagues. When the big leagues decided to try replacement players, it was like a feeding frenzy. Our phone was ringing off the hook. We sold about 70 players to big-league teams. A couple of teams called about wanting to sign guys we were about to cut. We called all our teams and said, 'Don't cut anyone! Let's see who the big leagues think can play and maybe we can make a few bucks off this.' We sold our players for $3,000 each. But some of the big-league teams were so cheap, they didn't even want to pay the three grand. The Indians were good, but I had one team offer me 375 bucks for a guy. Things like that made me as mad at the owners as I was at the stupid players."

The Indians signed Pete Kuld, who led the Northern League with 27 homers. Even though he played in Thunder Bay, Kuld always wore sunglasses. He had played as high as the Class AA level in the Oakland A's farm system. He also had played in Class A with the Indians. The Indians also bought three other players for $3,000 each. Wolff was so impressed with the Indians' willingness to bargain in good faith, that he threw in a player for free — a first baseman by the name of Mel Wearing.

"I saw (former Indian) Brett Butler saying that our guys should not have taken that chance to be replacements," Wolff said. "I wanted to throw up. Butler makes millions. He can afford to sit out. Besides, what has the Major League Players Association ever done for the career minor-leaguer? If the union really cared about our guys, they could have offered to use some of their pension money with players and coaches who have spent their lives in the minors. But they never did."

So the Indians and other teams had no trouble finding guys who wanted to play.

But how many of them could play?

When the Indians opened training camp in February of 1995 in Winter Haven, Fla., it was a strange sight. These were not the *real* Indians, but strangers in Cleveland uniforms. One coach pulled me over and said, "Wait until you get a load of Joe D. — and I mean, he is a load."

I checked the roster and Joe D. was Joe Demus, a catcher who was listed at 6-foot-2 and 189 pounds. There was no age next to his name. It turned out that asking replacement players for their ages was a futile exercise — most of them gave you their "baseball age," which was about five years short of the truth. So the Indians decided to just skip the whole issue.

"Says here that the guy weighs 189," I told the coach.

"He's supposed to weigh *what?*" asked the coach. "This guy has such a gut on him that, I swear, he'll have a heart attack in three days — if he lasts three days."

Others wondered if he would become the next Al Jones.

Jones became the first Tribe replacement player to do a TV interview. He told Lisa Bercu of WEWS Channel 5 that he had won 21 games in Taiwan in 1994. Yes, he said Taiwan, and I didn't even know they played pro baseball in Taiwan. Jones even had the baseball cards of himself to prove it, although the writing was Taiwanese so no one could verify his story.

All was well until the Indians had him take a physical. Then Al Jones, the 21-game winner from Taiwan, could not even lift his right arm above his head — arthritis. He was cut on the spot.

Joe Demus once was a Class A catcher for the Boston Red Sox. But he had spent the two years prior to becoming a replacement player delivering Italian food in Worthington, W.Va. Or, as the coach told me, "He must have eaten most of what he delivered."

Hart signed Demus "because he wrote a good letter saying he was a catcher with three years of minor league experience. We're always looking for catchers. We checked it out, and he really did play three years in the Boston farm system."

So Hart gave Demus what amounted to a one-day contract.

The Indians' first look at Demus The Player came in the batting cage. He said he was a switch-hitter, which was news to Hart and Mike Hargrove, who were watching him. The fact that Demus' lifetime minor league batting average was .193 with only one home run in three seasons

— well, that was news to them, too.

As he stood at home plate, Joe D. looked back over his shoulder at Hart and Hargrove, two guys who could change his life. He smashed the batting helmet down on top of his head and wiped the sweat from his brow. If he had ever been more nervous, he didn't know when. He swung at the first pitch, grunting as he fouled it straight down into his feet.

"Joe D., where you from?" asked Hargrove.

"West Virginia, sir," Demus replied.

"I figured there was something wrong with you," Hargrove said and then laughed. He knew that Demus' throat was so tight it felt like a fist, and Hargrove was trying to loosen him up.

Demus hit a little bit. Two balls even went over the fence, although he grunted as if he had been punched in the stomach each time he swung the bat.

He showed enough to remain on the field.

Next were the throwing drills. The first pitch came to Joe D. He dropped it — no throw to third base. The next pitch was caught cleanly, but he fired it over the third baseman's head. The third pitch was dropped again — no throw. The fourth pitch he caught but threw in the dirt.

"The poor guy is so nervous, I feel bad for him," Hart said.

Not as bad as Joe D. felt when he went to the next stop, the agility range. One look told Joe D. he was in trouble. He had to run backwards. He had to run sideways. He had to run in circles around orange cones.

Even on a good day, Joe D. can't run at all.

He was soaked with sweat, in a near panic. The Joe D. fat jokes had stopped. The coaches knew they were watching a man come to the realization that he didn't belong. He may have been a ballplayer once, but never again.

The best that could be said of Joe D. on the agility range is that he made it through without keeling over. He was called over by a few coaches. They spoke for about 30 seconds. Joe D. nodded and didn't say a word. He was 28 years old. He once had played pro ball, but he was exposed for what he was — a nice guy who delivers Italian food. In the Indians office, there was a one-way ticket to West Virginia waiting for him.

For Joe Demus, his spring was one day. Some of the other replacements had a full spring training, complete with exhibition games, including one at Jacobs Field. Hart and Hargrove tried to make the best of it. These were good guys who tried hard, but there were reasons they all had been cut at one time or another in their careers. As Hargrove observed, the more they played, the more their weaknesses were exposed.

There were days when Hargrove and Hart were convinced that there were indeed curses. How could they actually be heading into a season with a bunch of guys who had been cut from the Eastern League? After all the dues they paid with the likes of Albert Belle and Manny Ramirez, now they had to watch guys like Joe Demus?

Meanwhile, the best Indians team in 41 years sat at home — waiting. No one was sure what would happen. There were no signs of a settlement. The union was hanging together. The owners were coming to the realization that replacement ball wasn't going to sell.

In early April of 1995, there was no way to know that this would be the Indians' greatest season since 1954. Heck, most people had no idea that there would even be a season at all.

6

BACK IN CONTROL

April 27, 1995: After the strike and the possibility of a season with replacement players finally was over, the Indians began their quest for their first pennant in 41 years. Dennis Martinez took the mound in Texas, pitching six strong innings and allowing two runs as Cleveland beat Texas, 11-6. It was bombs away almost from the start. First Paul Sorrento and then Albert Belle, Eddie Murray, Manny Ramirez and Carlos Baerga all went deep, accounting for eight runs. As the Beacon Journal's Sheldon Ocker wrote, "At this rate, the Indians will hit 720 home runs this year. And yes, that's supposed to be funny, but maybe not that funny."

Early in spring training of 1995, Dennis Martinez told me he had a secret.

"Don't tell anybody," he whispered, "but I'm a grandfather."

Then Martinez laughed. After all, he was 40 years old and his dark hair was streaked with gray.

His 20-year-old daughter Erica showed up at a spring-training game and there was a bundle in her arms — her 7-month-old daughter. Martinez has a son, too, 21-year-old Dennis Martinez Jr., who pitched in the Tribe farm system in 1995.

Yes, Dennis Martinez is a man with adult children and a grandchild. A man who nearly lost his life to alcoholism, but managed to beat the bottle and also keep his 22-year marriage intact. A man who won at least 14 games in 11 different seasons. A man who, at the age of 40, was the ace of the Indians pitching staff.

"You gotta admit — I have a lot of experience," Martinez said with a laugh.

No denying that.

"But I know what people say," he said. "They talk about you getting to be 40 years old. Even if you have a good year, they think that you're old. They say, 'Yes, you did it last year, but you won't do it again.' "

Would Martinez do it again? That was one of the questions at the start of the 1995 season. He answered it in a decisive fashion — with a 12-5 record and a 3.08 ERA and by being named to the All-Star team.

"When I was young, I had a great arm. I don't have that anymore," he said. "But when I was young, they always said how I should win 20 games every year, but I didn't work hard or I was too dumb."

In the spring of 1979, Martinez and I were together in Miami, Fla. He was a 23-year-old pitcher with the Baltimore Orioles. I was a rookie baseball writer with the Baltimore Evening Sun. Ray Miller was Baltimore's pitching coach, and on the first day of camp he took me down to the bullpen where Martinez was warming up.

"Look at the fastball, look how it moves," Miller said as the ball popped into Dave Skaggs' glove. "Look at his slider, the bite on it. The ball just dives down. And his curve — Dennis has a great curve. Dennis is the whole package. He can be another Palmer."

In Baltimore, calling someone the next Jim Palmer was about the same as saying a young Tribe pitcher was another Bob Feller.

"That was a lot of expectations to put on me," Martinez said. "I was very young back then. I grew up in Nicaragua. Palmer was still on our staff, and I was supposed to be like him? It was too much to ask."

By his 23rd birthday, Martinez already had a 30-18 record in the majors. The Orioles of the 1960s and 1970s turned out one great pitcher after another — Dave McNally, Mike Cuellar, Mike Flanagan, Scott McGregor and Pat Dobson. Even pitchers such as Steve Stone who joined the Orioles in the late stages of their careers often won more games than ever before.

So why not expect greatness from Martinez?

"Physically, maybe they were right," he said. "But mentally, I just wasn't ready."

Martinez was the biggest-name ballplayer from Nicaragua, a real national hero in the Latin American country. Everywhere he traveled during the season, his countrymen would throw a party for Dennis, and Martinez discovered he liked to party back then.

He used booze as an escape and those who wanted to drink with him as an excuse to get drunk. Then he degenerated to the point where he drank by himself, stashing bottles in his hotel room. He spent much of his time at the ballpark wishing the game would end so he could get to those bottles.

By 1986, he should have been in his prime. Instead, he was back in the minor leagues. He was 31 years old. And he might have never returned to the majors if it hadn't been for Hank Peters.

Peters was the general manager of the Orioles from the late 1970s to 1987. In December of 1985, Peters wasn't just concerned that Martinez's pitching had taken a turn for the worse. He worried that Martinez's life was like a car careening out of control.

"Around Christmas time, Dennis had a one-car accident in Baltimore," Peters said. "He was drunk and was lucky he didn't kill himself."

Peters recalled Martinez's bloodshot eyes and his short attention span. He saw a man who seemed determined to live fast and die young.

"The accident gave us the opportunity to bring Dennis into our office and read him the riot act," Peters said. "We confronted him with the fact that he was an alcoholic and demanded that he get help."

At first, Martinez resisted. But Peters insisted that Martinez deal with his drinking.

"He wanted to take his family on a vacation to the Bahamas," Peters said. "We said that was fine, but when you come back, you go into rehab."

Martinez agreed and kept his word, spending close to two months at the Sheppard Pratt Hospital in Baltimore. When he was released, it was time for spring training. He was clean and sober, but not in shape to pitch.

After the rehabilitation, Peters was convinced that Martinez would be able to recapture the form that had made him a 15-game winner, good for 225 innings a year with the Orioles in the early 1980s.

"But I didn't know if it could happen in Baltimore," Peters said. "The fans were down on him after all his problems. He's sensitive and reacted to that. Sometimes a guy has to make a break with his past, so I figured the best thing to do was trade him."

During the 1986 season, Peters called every team in baseball about Martinez.

"No one but Montreal was interested, and we had to pay some of Dennis' salary for the Expos to take him," Peters said. "We got Rene Gonzales in return. It wasn't a good deal for the Orioles, but I wanted to give Dennis a fresh start in a new league."

Martinez made the most of it. Over his last six years with the Expos (1988-93), he cranked out about 15 victories and 220 innings a season. He often credited Peters as the man behind his comeback.

Peters left the Orioles to become the Tribe's president in 1987. It was Peters who hired current Indians general manager John Hart and farm director Dan O'Dowd. Peters also kept tabs on Martinez.

"A few years ago, Dennis was a free agent and we talked about signing him with the Indians," Peters said. "But Dennis said he felt some loyalty to Montreal, and he stayed with them."

Then, after the 1993 season, Martinez went on the free-agent market again. This time, the Tribe pushed harder to sign him. By then Peters had retired, turning the team over to Hart. But Peters remained in contact with Hart and Indians owner Dick Jacobs. He advised them to sign Martinez and Eddie Murray, who also was a former Oriole during Peters' regime.

"It's exciting for me to see the Indians get two players I've always considered to be my guys," Peters said. "And I always wanted to get Dennis back on my team, especially because of how proud I am of how he turned his life around."

The Dennis Martinez I saw with the Indians was a far different pitcher from the Dennis Martinez of 1979. His face was lined and leathery, a souvenir of too many late nights and too many empty bottles. But his body was in tremendous shape, in better shape than it had been when he was 23. Much of the time that Martinez used to spend drinking and nursing hangovers was now spent in the workout room, on the exercise bike, Stairmaster and treadmill.

On the mound, his fastball didn't quite have its old zip, but everything else in his arsenal was sharp.

"Now, most people would say that I am a smart pitcher," he said. "I don't throw as hard as I did, but I pitch better."

He proved that in 1994, posting an 11-6 record and a 3.52 ERA for the Tribe in that strike-shortened season. He threw a four-hitter at Comiskey Park against the White Sox. He tossed a two-hit, 7-0 victory over Boston at Fenway Park.

In 1995, he threw two more shutouts and had a 12-5 record and a 3.08 ERA.

Add up those two seasons, and Martinez's mark is 23-11 with a 3.30 ERA. He also averaged seven innings per start.

"I want the ball and can pitch a lot of innings," he said. "I learned pitching the right way with (Manager) Earl Weaver in Baltimore. That staff — we had Jim Palmer, Scotty McGregor, Mike Flanagan and myself.

We had a lot of competition. If McGregor threw a complete game one day, then I wanted to do the same the next — maybe even pitch a shutout. It was an attitude we have started to develop in Cleveland, where the pitchers all pull for each other, but also try to out-do each other. That is what makes a great pitching staff."

Martinez often was hurt and insulted by the gruff discipline imposed by Weaver and the Orioles. But these days he's become a walking textbook on the old Baltimore approach to pitching. He throws strikes. He fields his position well. He likes to surprise you with a breaking pitch early in the count.

"But a couple of times a game, I can still throw the fastball that really makes the glove pop," he said.

Most of his fastballs are in the 87 mph range, but he'll reach back for a 92 mph lightning bolt in stormy situations. He also is willing to pitch inside. That also comes from Weaver and the Orioles.

Many young pitchers refuse to pitch inside. They worry about hitting batters. They also worry that if they don't get the ball far enough inside, the hitters will hit it over the fence.

Martinez insists that he never actually throws at anyone, even though he ranked second in the American League in 1995 with 12 hit batters.

"OK, there was this time when I was pitching amateur ball in Nicaragua," he said. "One of our infielders was getting ready to catch a pop-up, and a baserunner goes by and elbows (the infielder) right in the head. I saw that and said, 'I'm gonna get him.' I just waited until he came to bat."

What happened?

"I threw four pitches — two inside and two behind the guy," Martinez said. "I never threw harder in my life, but I missed him all four times, and he walked."

That was the only time?

"(Former Boston first baseman) George Scott thought I threw at him," he said. "It was when I was a rookie (with the Orioles in 1977). I was just trying to throw inside, but Scott, he dropped his big bat and came running at me. He was 270 pounds — a big, ugly man — and I was just a scared, skinny kid from Nicaragua. I turned and ran into center field. If (Oriole first baseman) Lee May hadn't tackled him, that Scott would have killed me.

"Back then, everybody made fun of me because I ran away. They said I was a big chicken. They said I should have stood and fought Scott. If I did that . . . instead of pitching at 40, everybody would be saying what a good career Dennis Martinez would have had if he hadn't tried to fight George Scott."

Still, the incident messed him up.

"For the next seven years, I was afraid to pitch inside," Martinez said. "I kept thinking that if I hit someone, they'd come hurt me."

Almost every story Martinez tells about his life draws back to his days with the Orioles and his decision to stop drinking.

"I'm not afraid to pitch inside anymore," he said. "I never throw at a hitter. When I do hit a guy, it usually is in the hip or the side. I don't throw at his head. But you have to let these hitters know that the plate belongs to both you and him. You share it. I don't let them take the inside corner away from me."

Weaver demanded that his pitchers stake a claim to the inside corner, and you do that by throwing the ball there, and throwing it hard. During his alcoholism rehabilitation, Martinez realized that he could pitch inside.

"I knew that if I did hit someone, I didn't mean it to happen," he said. "It's really not my fault. I stopped worrying about it."

He insists that the duel between a hitter and a pitcher is really a war over real estate.

"The hitters are like monsters," Martinez said. "They want to take the plate away from you. They stand real close to the plate and gobble it up. I've seen good young pitchers driven out of the big leagues because they just kept throwing the ball outside all the time. Why give half of home plate to the hitter? If you pitch inside, if you miss the corner, you better miss inside by a foot — not over the plate, or the hitter will kill you. That is why you sometimes hit guys. They are guessing you'll throw outside, and you throw a little more inside than you mean to. It's an accident. As long as you know in your heart that you're not trying to hit someone, you should have nothing to worry about."

Martinez relishes his role as the veteran pitcher, storyteller and giver of advice.

"Sometimes I think (about) what I might have accomplished if I didn't have the drinking problem," he said. "Would I have won 20 games in a season? Would I have 300 wins by now? (He had 231 after the 1995 season). But I still made three All-Star teams. I've pitched a perfect game. Maybe I needed to go through all that to be a better person and pitcher now."

In 1995, it seemed that every start with Martinez was an adventure.

When he pitched and won on Father's Day, he spent his post-game press conference talking about his son, Dennis Jr., who had just signed with the Tribe. He talked about how it was his dream to play on the same team with his son. His eyes were moist as he played the role of the proud papa.

In mid-June, Martinez pitched a game with torn cartilage in his left knee. He took a line drive in the chest off the bat of Baltimore's Brady Anderson in the fifth inning. His heart stopped, he said.

"I can show you my chest," he said. "It's all black and blue.

"After I was hit, they told me to sit down on the mound, but I was afraid I'd never get up again. I thought I might have a heart attack, and my heart just stopped. Then my heart was pounding, and I thought I was going to stop breathing."

As you listen to Martinez, you realize that his story keeps changing. Sometimes his heart stopped beating . . . then his heart pounded . . . yes, his heart was alive after all . . . then he was convinced he was going to stop breathing.

The bottom line? A line drive knocked Martinez down, but not out. He stayed on the mound for nine innings, racking up his 28th career shutout while beating the Orioles.

In a quiet moment, Martinez will tell you, "My arm is a gift from God." He will tell you how on the day Mickey Mantle died his wife Luz Marina called him and said, "That could have been you." He will tell you how he thanks the Lord that he was able to stop drinking before his body was ravaged like Mantle's.

"It is like I had two careers," he said. "I don't dwell on it, but I remember all the bad things people said about me and who said them back when I was having my problems. I know they never thought I'd come back, and they sure never thought I'd be pitching at 40. Sometimes I see those people and I want to tell them to kiss my butt, but I just let it go. Why go back into the past again?"

7

LETTING HIS LEGS DO THE TALKING

May 7, 1995: It took the Indians six hours and 36 minutes to beat the Minnesota Twins. It took them 17 innings. Both teams combined to use 132 baseballs. There were 17 pitchers in the game; they threw the ball 590 times to home plate. The game finally ended when Kenny Lofton drove in the winning run with a base hit to right field. The Indians would have liked to have mobbed Lofton, but they were too tired. They were just glad to win, and the victory in the longest game (time-wise) in team history raised the Tribe's record to 6-4.

How often does anything come as advertised?

The vegetable slicer will cut and dice your fingers. The miracle diet seems to add inches to your waistline. And that great "pre-owned" car is really nothing more than someone else's clunker. That is why it is a shock to go back and read what was said on the day the Indians traded for Kenny Lofton.

"We project him as an impact-type player who has a chance to help us this year," said General Manager John Hart.

That was on Dec. 10, 1991, when Hart sent minor league catcher Eddie Taubensee and right-handed pitcher Willie Blair to Houston for Lofton and a utility infielder named Dave Rohde.

Lofton was 24 and had played a mere 20 games in the majors, batting .203 with only one extra-base hit in 74 at-bats. The Astros were not impressed. Sure, they liked Lofton, but they didn't see him as "the prototype leadoff hitter and centerfielder."

But Hart did, and that was exactly how he characterized Lofton on the day of the deal.

And there was more.

"There are certain players whom you know have talent and they give it to you every game," Hart continued. "You walk away from the ballpark excited after seeing them. I never walked away from a ballpark without being excited by what I saw from Kenny Lofton."

Remember, this was back in December of 1991. Lofton was considered by many scouts to be a basketball player trying to learn baseball. He was an athlete. He was a sprinter. But he wasn't a hitter, and he certainly wasn't the "prototype" leadoff man.

If the Astros had thought so, they never would have traded him.

Houston was in the market for a catcher, and Taubensee was highly regarded. In fact, Hart tried to keep him out of the deal, but the Astros insisted. Hart hesitated for a moment, trying to find other names that would satisfy the Astros. But Houston said, "We need a catcher, and if you don't give us one for Lofton, another team will."

Tribe batting coach Charlie Manuel had managed the Indians Class AAA team in Colorado Springs in 1991; it was in the same Pacific Coast League where Lofton hit 17 triples — more than any player in any pro league in 1991. Manuel told Hart about how he hated to manage against Lofton, how Lofton's speed disrupted the game and drove pitchers to distraction. Farm Director Dan O'Dowd had one glowing scouting report after another about Lofton. Manuel and O'Dowd told Hart what he already knew: Lofton was special; go get him.

Hart did.

Lofton went to spring training with the Indians in 1992. He had to beat out Alex Cole and Glenallen Hill for the center-field job. Cole could hit but needed to wear a helmet when he played the outfield. Fans wondered why Cole didn't have his glasses checked as it often seemed like fly balls were about to hit him in the head. He had a quick first step, but it usually was in the wrong direction. If the ball went deep, he came in. If the ball was short, he took a step back. It was as if he guessed where the ball was hit then looked up and tried to find it. As for Glenallen Hill, he had as much chance of playing center for the Tribe as he did starting at quarterback for the Browns.

Lofton was the guy, and that was fine with him. One of the ways Lofton motivates himself is to decide that someone has "dissed" or insulted him in some manner. In this case, he was enraged at Houston "for giving up on me." He spent his first year with the Tribe determined to prove the Astros wrong, to rub the trade in their faces.

Hart and his staff had appreciated Lofton's fire from a distance when they scouted him in the Pacific Coast League. When they came closer to the flame, they liked it even more. A guy who wanted to play that bad — who wanted to prove himself so much — well, that was exactly the type of young player the Indians needed to pump some life into the comatose franchise.

Of all the players on the Indians roster, perhaps the most difficult for the media is Kenny Lofton.

Many fans are surprised to hear that. They figure it would be Belle, given Albert's very public explosions. But Belle either insults you or speaks at great length and with insight. There is nothing in between. With one question, you know whether Belle is having one of his good or bad days. And Belle on a good day is engaging and worth hearing.

Lofton is like a flyweight boxer who never lets down his guard. To him, everyone is a pitcher who wants to pick him off first base. When he talks, his eyes bounce from one end of the room to the other, as if he were expecting a sneak attack.

"Controversy is my big fear," he said. "I don't want to say anything that will be controversial, and reporters like to get you into that."

Lofton took several communications courses at the University of Arizona, and he believes that he has this media business figured out. He is convinced that reporters want players to say outrageous or stupid things so that they'll make headlines, and headlines sell newspapers and get raises for reporters.

There is some truth to Lofton's theory, but the guys who cover the Indians can't afford to make up things and engage in scorch-the-earth journalism. The three major writers who travel with the team — the Plain Dealer's Paul Hoynes, Jim Ingram of the Lake County News-Herald and the Beacon Journal's Sheldon Ocker — have all been covering the team for at least 10 years. All are respected, and none of them are known as "rip men" who take cheap shots at players. Lofton has received little criticism from anyone since joining the Tribe because he has been such a terrific player.

But he remains withdrawn. If it were just with the media, that would be fine. But there are times when Lofton throws up a stone wall to his superiors.

This is especially true when he has an injury.

"Kenny just doesn't like to talk about being hurt," Manager Mike

Hargrove said. "You ask him how he feels and he'll say, 'Fine.' He keeps it to himself. Sometimes, it is hard to know what Kenny is thinking."

There were times in the 1995 season when Hart or Hargrove tried to take a reading on Lofton's injuries — he had both a sore back and a pulled muscle in his rib cage — and Lofton barely said three words to them. He acted as if they were prying reporters, trying to expose one of his weaknesses.

But Hart and Hargrove needed to know exactly how Lofton felt so they could determine whether he should go on the disabled list or whether he would be all right in a few days. When a player lives off his legs as Lofton does, then it is critical for the manager to know exactly how well Lofton can run. What if Lofton is hurt and can't steal a base, but Hargrove needs a stolen base in a critical situation? The manager must have that information.

But it just isn't in Lofton's nature to reveal much of himself. One Tribe official said talking to Lofton when he's hurting "can be like extracting wisdom teeth."

Lofton's favorite response to a question is a shrug and a throwaway line such as, "Don't worry about it."

Lofton's suspicion of strangers probably has a lot to do with how he was raised.

He weighed only 3 pounds at birth. His mother was a teen-ager, who was terrified that she would drop the tiny infant. So his grandmother made a pillow, and it was on that little pillow that Kenny Lofton was carried during the first few months of his life.

He was raised by his grandmother, Rosie Person, who lived in the housing projects of East Chicago, Ind. While Rosie kept her apartment clean and neat, the project was a slum — a filthy, dangerous, dirt-poor tenement in a Godforsaken part of the world between Gary and Chicago. Rosie's husband, a steelworker, had died in 1960. He had felt like he was getting the flu, but he kept working. The flu became pneumonia and it killed him. Rosie was left with seven children to raise on a Social Security check.

While Lofton's mother, Annie, attended high school, it was Rosie Person who took care of young Kenny. After graduating, Annie moved to Alabama and Kenny remained with his grandmother. For Lofton, this was a blessing because his grandmother was a loving woman, a strong moral presence.

Lofton doesn't smoke or drink. He has never been in any trouble with the law. Though he grew up in a neighborhood where crime was a way of life — the path of least resistance — Lofton took his own far-more-demanding road.

When he was a child, Lofton's grandmother began to experience vision problems, which would become so severe that she was nearly blind by the time he attended college. Her failing eyesight prevented her from working outside of their home. But Rosie didn't ask for sympathy and had little patience with whiners. She believed that you took what God gave you and you made the best of it. That could be the source of Lofton's unwillingness to admit that any injury has slowed him down, even briefly.

For a while, the family rented the basement of a home in East Chicago. The floor was concrete; the walls were brick. It was a cold, poor place. Lofton seldom had new toys or clothes. He knew that whatever he was given, he had better protect. He lived in a place where other kids liked to steal or destroy things. In that environment, Lofton had to feel that it was him and his grandmother against the world.

As a child, Lofton had promised Rosie Person that he would do something special, that he would make enough money so she could live in a nice house and a safe place. She told Kenny just to grow up healthy and strong and do the right things.

Rosie loved baseball and as her eyesight grew worse, the radio became her companion. She loved listening to games, especially the Cubs in the afternoon. When Harry Caray would sing *Take Me Out to the Ball Game*, she and young Kenny both would stand up and sing along.

She believed sports were good for her grandson, and encouraged him to play Little League. He went on to play through high school, and, as a senior, he batted .414.

By high school, Lofton also was playing guard for Washington High School's basketball team. That 3-pound infant had grown into a 6-footer with a 40-inch vertical leap. He was an all-state selection as a guard during his senior year, and major college basketball coaches began visiting East Chicago, talking to Lofton and his grandmother.

Lofton picked Arizona. He and his grandmother both liked the gray-haired, quiet Lute Olson. They thought Tucson was a clean, safe city — a perfect tonic to the dirt and crime of East Chicago. Lofton also realized that Arizona was just building a good basketball team and that he had a chance to come in and go to work on the ground floor. For years, Arizona's basketball had been a farce, but Olson was determined to change all that.

Lofton wanted to be a part of that program. In fact, you can draw a comparison between Lofton being one of Olson's early recruits at Arizona and his trade to the Indians — in both places, he became a key part of a team that surprised the sports world.

Lofton played on the same Arizona basketball team with Steve Kerr, Anthony Cook and Sean Elliott, and all three went on to play in the NBA. He was a sixth man on that 1988 team that went to the NCAA Final Four. He went to Arizona with the idea of playing baseball and basketball, but discovered that basketball dominated much of his time.

So baseball was put on hold.

But in the spring of 1988, he tried out for Arizona's baseball team. He appeared in five games, mostly as a pinch runner. He batted twice. There was no reason to assume that this guy would even play pro baseball, much less make an American League All-Star team.

But a Houston scout saw Lofton practice a few times. Clark Crist is a former Arizona player, and when he stopped by to watch his alma mater play an intra-squad game, he was intrigued by Lofton's speed. He knew Lofton was a basketball player, but had no idea he played baseball until that day at practice.

What Crist saw was a runner and jumper in a baseball uniform. Lofton had a hitch in his swing and seldom made solid contact. In the field, he seemed to break in the wrong direction when the ball was hit, but he was so quick that he'd turn around and make the play anyway.

Crist believed that if you took a guy who was a great natural athlete and who had a burning desire, you could make him into a baseball player. That was the essence of his scouting report to the Astros, who drafted Lofton in the 17th round in June of 1988.

Lofton still had one more year of eligibility left in basketball, but the NCAA had passed a rule allowing a player to be an amateur in one sport, and a professional in another. So Lofton signed with the Astros.

He batted only .214 at Class A Auburn in the New York-Penn League. He was rusty and raw, striking out 51 times in 187 at-bats, a frightening ratio.

But he stole 26 bases in 48 games. He could run, and the Astros wanted to work with him full-time. At the same time, Lofton was practicing basketball (especially his jump shot) three times a week to prepare for his senior year at Arizona.

"I wasn't prepared for pro baseball," he said. "But the Astros told me that speed was something you can't teach. In my first year or two, my organizations. He also has passed out meals on Thanksgiving and donated a sizable chunk of cash to help build a Baptist church in his old neighborhood. He was honored as the "1994 East Chicagoan of the Year," and there is a street in that town named Kenny Lofton Lane.

Guess who lives on Kenny Lofton Lane.

It's his grandmother, Rosie Person. She is out of the projects and in a new home. Just as Lofton came as advertised to the Tribe, Lofton kept his word to the woman who raised him.

mind was on two sports. Once I began to concentrate on baseball, I got my career going."

He returned to Arizona for his senior year, averaging 6.5 points. He led the team in assists and steals. ESPN basketball commentator Dick Vitale made Lofton one of his finalists for "Dunk of the Year," screaming about one of Lofton's slams despite Lofton being only a 6-footer.

Lofton believes that he could have been an NBA player, that the disciplined Arizona system didn't highlight his skills and athletic ability. He has often said that if he had played for Jerry Tarkanian at the University of Nevada at Las Vegas, he might indeed have been in the NBA.

Instead, Lofton gave himself over to baseball in the summer of 1989. Hitting wasn't easy, but he stole 40 bases in 56 games. More importantly, the Astros were excited by Lofton's attitude. This guy didn't think he had it made. He was open to instruction and knew "my mechanics needed a lot of work."

Lofton progressed through the Astros farm system. So often, these "natural athletes" don't learn how to play baseball. They are so accustomed to relying on their athletic gifts that they don't believe they need what amounts to remedial work. They often disdain the bunt, even though it is a powerful weapon for a guy with speed. But Lofton loved to bunt. He practiced his bunting as much as his hitting.

When Lofton was promoted to Houston for the final 20 games of the 1991 season, the Astros made a critical scouting mistake. They looked at his .203 batting average and the 19 strikeouts in 74 at-bats, and they used that as an indicator that he would never be a primo offensive player in the big leagues.

In their defense, it often appeared as if a good inside fastball would knock the bat right out of Lofton's hands. But Lofton's late start in baseball meant that he would need more time than the average prospect to adjust. His documented ability to adapt to the different levels of minor league competition was an indicator that he should be able to do the same in the majors.

But the Astros had a centerfielder named Steve Finley, who batted .285 for them in 1991. They decided he was their man. They also weren't thrilled that Lofton refused to take part in the team's winter instructional league program. But Lofton went back to Arizona in the off-season to complete his degree in mass media and communications — to fulfill a promise he'd made his grandmother.

All these factors — the Astros' need of a catcher, Lofton's early struggles in the majors, the Indians' excellent scouting and Lofton's tenacity

— led to one of the best trades in the history of the Indians franchise.

Having the modern player's usual view of history, Kenny Lofton has never heard of Tris Speaker, but Lofton is the closest thing the Indians have ever had to The Gray Eagle, which was Speaker's nickname. Speaker was the Tribe's player/manager in 1920, when they won the World Series. He was a Hall of Famer, a lifetime .344 hitter over 20 seasons. He also was a great fielder, credited with being the first centerfielder to play shallow and dare the batter to hit the ball over his head.

In fact, Speaker positioned himself so close that he would catch a pick-off throw *at second base* from the pitcher. In 1918, he recorded two *unassisted* double plays when he ran in, caught a line drive near second base, then tagged the runner before he could return to second. His Hall of Fame statue reads: "The greatest centerfielder of his day."

Since then, the Indians have had some terrific centerfielders. Larry Doby was superb. Rick Manning was a mediocre hitter, but a Gold Glove in center and fearless when it came to challenging walls and fences to take away possible home runs. But none of them compared to Speaker — or even Lofton.

Lofton hit .285 as a rookie with the Tribe in 1992. Then it was .325 in 1993, .349 in 1994 and .310 in 1995. By the end of the 1995 season, he had led the American League in stolen bases in three of the four previous seasons and had won three Gold Gloves.

This is Lofton at his best: When he was a rookie, he faced Jack Morris, who was then with Toronto and coming off a year when he was the 1991 World Series hero.

In his first at-bat, Lofton bunted. Morris picked up the ball, walked back to the mound and angrily kicked the rubber.

In his second at-bat, Lofton bunted again — for another hit. Morris just stared at the rookie. He took this bunting as an insult, especially bunting twice.

In his third at-bat, Morris unleashed a fastball that nearly chopped off Lofton's legs. He hit the dirt, then calmly stood up and brushed himself off. Morris was telling Lofton, "You want to bunt on me, well, I'll break your kneecap."

Morris delivered again and Lofton bunted — again. Morris actually fielded this roller and threw Lofton out at first. But the Indians were thrilled to see Lofton refuse to sacrifice any part of his game to a veteran and intimidating pitcher.

The same toughness that carried Lofton out of the East Chicago projects can be seen on the field. Lofton will run the bases with abandon, sliding head- or feet-first — not worrying about injuries or hard tags, just trying to beat the throw. He also will throw his body against a wall to make a catch in deep center.

How many players are capable of a home run, a stolen base, a bunt single and a Gold Glove-caliber catch — all in the same game?

Lofton has done that more than a few times in four years with the Tribe.

He also plays in anger. After his first season, he was angry when he was passed over for Milwaukee's Pat Listach for 1992 American League Rookie of the Year. Lofton lives in Tucson, and when he heard the news, he drove his car up a mountain outside of town and screamed.

"I looked over the whole city and yelled as loud as I could," he said. "It was my way of letting out my aggression . . . Justice wasn't done. The writers taking the award away from me were taking money out of my pocket."

In his second season, Toronto Manager Cito Gaston passed over him when picking reserves for the American League All-Star team. Again, that was enough to make Lofton scream.

Since then, he has become even more withdrawn from the press, despite that communications degree from Arizona. He does several press conferences a year with a group of children called "Kenny's Kids" and reveals a very engaging side. These are 50 inner-city children in Cleveland for whom he buys tickets for Saturday home games. He also works with some youth groups in the Cleveland and Chicago areas.

But he can turn sullen, seemingly for no reason.

Perhaps it has to do with growing up in a housing project. There are few places on Earth more violent and threatening to a young black male than a housing project in East Chicago. A kid in that environment is constantly told to trust no one, and those on the streets do things to drive that message home. Lofton has seen so many lives destroyed in so many ways, that perhaps he wants to make sure that no one or nothing sidetracks him.

So there are times when he keeps his distance — not just from the media but from fans and even his bosses.

It's too bad that Lofton doesn't let down his guard more often, because he sometimes gives the impression that he believes the whole world is out to steal his jacket. While he now makes his home in Tucson, he still spends a lot of time in East Chicago, appearing at several youth

8

LEARNING TO SAVE THE DAY

May 31, 1995: Jose Mesa came out of the bullpen to pitch the ninth inning and preserve the Indians' 6-3 victory over the Chicago White Sox. It was Mesa's fourth save in four days, and it established him as the ruler of the Tribe bullpen. The Indians ended the month of May with a 21-9 record, and Mesa had saved 11 of those 21 victories.

Show up at Jacobs Field about three hours before a game, and you'll find Jose Mesa running. Around and around he goes, wearing a headband with a long white tail that flaps behind him like a flag in the breeze. He'll also be decked out in a Bill Belichick-model garbage bag for a shirt and a pair of shorts.

Mesa laps the ballpark. Then he runs sprints in the outfield.

The Indians relief pitcher changes his program slightly, but he works out virtually every day, running at least three to four miles. At 6-foot-3 and 220 pounds, Mesa is a bull of a man with a barrel chest. But his regimen has turned that body to muscle, and it probably has a lot to do with his 98 mph fastball.

"I gotta do it," he said. "My goal is to be able to pitch every day if they need me. No doubt about it, there has not been one day this season when I've been tired."

"No doubt about it" is Mesa's favorite phrase, and there were no doubts about Mesa in 1995. He saved a team-record 46 games. He had a sparkling 1.13 earned-run average, the lowest ever by an Indians pitcher. Only twice did he fail to hold leads. When Mesa pitched, the Indians' record was 60-2.

There are even more numbers about Mesa, but the point worth remembering is that Mesa's emergence as a star moved the Indians from being a good team to a great one — something that's still hard for many longtime Tribe fans to believe. Even General Manager John Hart was shocked by Mesa's season, and Hart had more faith in him than anyone else.

"For all of his career, Jose had a great arm," Hart said. "That was why I traded for him back in 1992. It was a pure potential deal. He threw so hard, that he should have been a good pitcher, even though he wasn't one at the time. And in 1992 we weren't a very good team, so we had time to wait and see if he developed."

The Baltimore Orioles had Mesa for six years (from 1987 to 1992), but gave up on him.

"If I had stayed with the Orioles, I'd be out of baseball right now," Mesa said. "They didn't think I could pitch. Sometimes, I was their fifth starter. Then they got mad at me and put me in the bullpen, but didn't pitch me much. I guess they didn't like me."

Given the fact that all the Orioles took was a non-prospect named Kyle Washington in a trade, Mesa's self-scouting report sounds accurate. His record in Baltimore was 13-24.

But Mesa is more than numbers. He seems to have a story about everything.

"Know what else happened after I got traded?" he asked. "They broke into my house. This 18-year-old girl in the neighborhood, she heard I was traded. She and her boyfriend broke a window and moved in."

Moved in?

"They were there for a week. They ate my food. They slept in my bed. They had friends over and had a party. The guy, he wore my Orioles T-shirts, my cap, my pants, even my shoes. When the police finally caught him, the guy was dressed up as me. He had a shirt on that said 'Mesa.' "

They also stole his car.

"It was just a little bitty Hyundai," he said. "Some boys, they act crazy, you know? They put him in jail for a month."

If Mesa had any doubts about coming to Cleveland, the robbery convinced him that it was time for a new address.

Mesa's journey to Cleveland began in 1982 when he signed with the Toronto Blue Jays. He was only 15 and living outside of a town called Azua, in a rural area of the Dominican Republic.

"The day I signed my first pro contract, I was working on our farm," he said. "A friend of mine drove up on his motorbike. I was picking sweet potatoes, and he told me that the Blue Jays were having a tryout camp in town. I grabbed my glove, and jumped on the back of that motorbike with him and rode to town."

Mesa said he was an outfielder.

"The scouts put a stopwatch on me and I ran only a 7.4 in the 60-yard dash," he said. "They told me that I was too slow."

The Blue Jays scouts were looking for pitchers, so Mesa said that he could pitch, too. Anything for a contract. Anything for a way off the farm. Anything for a chance to play baseball in America.

"I never had pitched a game in my life," he said. "But I stood on the mound and threw as hard as I could. They had a radar gun and I threw the ball about 88 miles per hour."

At 15, Mesa was already 6-foot-3. He had sticks for arms and legs — you'd never believe how skinny he was, given the linebacker build he sports today. The scouts knew that he was young and that he'd fill out his frame. And 88 mph was fast for a kid who obviously had no idea about how to pitch.

A Toronto scout showed up at Mesa's home.

Jose Mesa is one of 25 children. You read that right, although Mesa will sometimes change the number when he tells the story.

"There were so many; it was hard to keep track," he said.

His father had 10 children from his first marriage. Then he had 15 more children with his second wife, Maria, who is Mesa's mother.

"There were kids spread out over 30 years, so there never were that many in the house all at once," he said. "But I do know that I was No. 12 of the 15 kids."

Anyway, the scout asked Maria Mesa if she thought a $3,000 bonus was fair. Did she want her son to play baseball for the Toronto Blue Jays?

She had no idea where Canada was, but knew that many grown men don't make $3,000 a year in the Dominican Republic.

"Where do I sign?" she asked.

With that, Mesa started on the very long road to Cleveland.

Mesa began his days with the Blue Jays at a camp for young prospects.

"After I signed, the Blue Jays sent me to a camp in a part of the Dominican where they had mountains," he recalled. "We'd get up at 7 a.m. and run through those mountains. That was where I learned about conditioning and working hard. After the mountains, running around Jacobs Field is easy."

Those who played well in a two-month tryout were sent to Bradenton, Fla., where the Blue Jays had a rookie-league team.

"When I went to Bradenton, I was 16 and I didn't even know enough English to order a French fry," he said.

Actually, "French fries" were two of the first words that Mesa learned, and he ordered them constantly during that first year in the Class A Gulf Coast League.

Mesa threw hard, but he was raw. He didn't know how to use his body to gain maximum leverage as he threw and get more speed on his fastball. He didn't know how to hold runners on base. He didn't know how to make the ball curve or sink. It is shorter to say what Mesa did know about pitching: throw as hard as you can for as long as you can.

Even when Mesa finally made the majors — the year was 1987 and he had been traded to Baltimore — he was still a one-trick pitcher.

"I threw hard," he said. "I had a curve, but it wasn't very good."

By 1987, Mesa was 22. He had put more than 200 pounds of muscle on that 6-foot-3 frame. His fastball speed was near 95 mph.

"I was a starter and I'd throw 130 pitches a game, and most of them were balls," he said, laughing.

The Orioles were fascinated by his arm strength, but frustrated by his control problems and his inability to grasp the fundamentals of pitching. They waited six years for Mesa to find himself, and then finally traded him to the Tribe during the 1992 All-Star break.

Mesa had been a starter in the minors and with the Orioles. In 1992 and 1993, the Indians also used him that way. And he continued to lose more games than he won.

Before spring training in 1994, the Indians had a staff meeting. Former pitching coach Phil Regan talked about how the team needed a reliever to replace the late Steve Olin.

"Why not try Jose?" Regan asked. "Tell him to come in for an inning or two, throw nothing but fastballs and sliders. Make pitching simple for him."

Hart loved new ideas, and he immediately latched onto this one. Mesa in the bullpen had been in the back of his mind. Of course, on any given day, there are 25 different ideas rolling around in the brain of John Hart.

"It made sense to me," Hart said. "Jose could never master an off-speed pitch. I don't care how hard you throw, if you are a starter, eventually you are going to need some type of change-up or slow curve just to keep the hitters off-balance over the course of a game."

Hargrove listened to this and thought, "Why not?" He had nothing else in the bullpen. He liked Eric Plunk — another flame-thrower — but Plunk never seemed comfortable pitching in the ninth inning with the game on his shoulders. Plunk was more effective in the seventh and eighth innings, working as the set-up man, a bridge between the starter and the ninth-inning closer. Hargrove pitched the idea to Mesa, who wasn't especially receptive.

Mesa viewed the move as a demotion. He thought the Indians didn't believe he had the right stuff to start, and they were pushing him into the bullpen, where he could be forgotten and lost. He was a bit depressed by how his career was going. He was 28 in the spring of 1994, and he still had not established himself in the majors.

"I always work hard," he said. "I always throw hard, too. But guys would say to me, 'Jose, with your arm, how do those guys hit you?' I'd tell them that the hitter does his job, too. But, sometimes, it made me sad. I wanted to pitch better, but it just didn't happen."

He knew that some people thought he had a million-dollar arm and a 10-cent head. He heard other pitchers say, "Jose, I wish I had your stuff. I'd never lose a game."

Mesa was not a party guy. He valued his body and was in tremendous physical condition. He tried to listen to his coaches.

The more he thought about the bullpen, the more he asked himself, "Why not?"

When the 1994 season opened, Mesa was the closer, the man brought into the game in the ninth inning to hold a lead.

He couldn't do it. Six times Manager Mike Hargrove brought Mesa into a save situation. Only twice did he come through.

Mesa lost confidence. Whispers were that he didn't have the poise and/or the guts to handle the pressure. Hargrove switched him to middle relief, and Mesa often pitched well, but it was usually in games where the Indians were behind and the pressure was off.

After the 1994 season, there was no reason to believe this guy would become the premier relief pitcher in all of baseball only a year later.

Mesa's contract was up after the 1994 season. Hart had a long talk with him.

"Jose, I still think you can be a closer," he said. "We need someone to do it, and with your arm — why not?"

Hart formulated a plan. He would give Mesa a two-year, $1.85 million contract; Mesa liked the sound of that security. Hart knew that Mesa planned to pitch winter ball in the Dominican Republic.

"Do that," he said. "But Jose, pitch out of the bullpen. Work on being a closer."

Mesa was 7-for-7 in save situations in the Dominican Republic, and the scouting reports were glowing. He was coming into games and just blowing people away.

As the 1995 season opened, Hart and Hargrove hoped Mesa would be their closer, but it was hard to count on him. So they planned to give young Paul Shuey a long look. And Hart was considering trades for veteran relievers such as Rick Aguilera, Dennis Eckersley and Bryan Harvey.

Eckersley was interested in coming to Cleveland, where he began his career, but the Oakland A's wanted Manny Ramirez in the deal. No way, Hart said. Not for a 40-year-old pitcher.

Harvey and Aguilera came with high price tags. Teams wanted at least two top pitching prospects such as Julian Tavarez, Albie Lopez or Chad Ogea. Hart didn't want to trade away the future. He also didn't want to take on a $3 million salary (that's what Aguilera and Harvey earned), so he decided to sit tight and watch Mesa In Relief: Year Two.

Mesa insisted he would be the man in the bullpen. He used his favorite phrase, "no doubt about it." He talked about how well he pitched in winter ball, but that impressed few people. Heck, former Indian Victor Cruz was virtually unhittable in the Dominican Republic during the winter. Come the regular season, however, and he was called "Cruise Missile" because of all the rockets he gave up to opposing hitters.

But it turned out that Mesa was right — a month into the season, there were no more doubts about him. It was as if at the age of 29 and after 13 years of pro ball, he finally had found his place.

"We had a stretch early in the season where I pitched him four days in a row," Hargrove said. "On the third day, his fastball was 96 mph and his slider was 88 mph. He's a horse."

Veteran Tony Pena often caught Mesa early in the season. When he saw something he didn't like, Pena would run to the mound and scream at him in Spanish.

"One time, Tony hit me in the head with his glove, right in the middle of the game," Mesa said. "Tony can be a crazy man. Other times, he throws the ball back at me so hard, I think he's trying to kill me."

"I do that to bring Jose's head back into the game," Pena said. "He has no idea how good he can be. The only guy I've caught who throws as hard as him is Roger Clemens."

Mesa kept throwing hard, and the hitters kept going down. On Aug. 20, 1995, he notched his 37th consecutive save — a major league record — as he pitched the ninth inning of the Tribe's 8-5 victory over Oakland. In that game, several of his pitches were clocked at 98 mph.

If you want to know why the Indians ran away with the Central Division championship — well, the biggest reason was Mesa.

"At the start of the year, he was our wild card," Hart said. "And he came up an ace."

Tribe fans latched onto Mesa, standing and cheering wildly whenever the bullpen door opened to start the ninth inning and Mesa strutted to the mound.

"I hear the fans every time," he said. "You'd have to be deaf not to hear those people."

Mesa has five children, and a couple of them are usually in the dressing room after games. He interrupted his press conference after his major league-record 37th save to change the diaper of 2-year-old Jose Jr.

"Jose is a good family man who is one of the best players we have when it comes to making personal appearances for charity," said Allen Davis, the Indians director of community relations. "Jose has had a tremendous amount of success, but none of it has gone to his head. He appreciates everything he has now."

Before the 1995 season, Mesa had a 34-45 record and a 4.89 ERA in the majors with only two saves. He had never made an All-Star team, not even in the minors. Then, like a bolt of lightning, he had the best season that any Cleveland reliever has ever had.

"I just think that Jose began to believe in himself," Hart said. "He saved a couple of games early in the season, and suddenly he said, 'I can do this.' He always had a great arm; now he's making it work for him."

Every winter, Mesa returns to the Dominican Republic.

"I can't wait to go back this year," he said at the end of the 1995 season. "Before, people say, 'There goes Jose Mesa, I think he's a ballplayer.' It was no big deal. But now, I have been getting faxes and letters from home. Whenever I get a save, they put my picture in the (Dominican) newspapers. They write nice stories about me. After the year I've had and all the games we've won, I think people will be very glad to see me now. It makes me feel good inside, to have my people respect me. That means so much — to work hard and then have people respect you."

9

PLAYING WITH THE BALL

June 12, 1995: The Indians beat Baltimore, 4-3. Charles Nagy was the winning pitcher. Jose Mesa saved his 15th consecutive game and Wayne Kirby had two hits. The Indians' lead in the Central Division was 7½ games. Few fans noticed Omar Vizquel. He played short and didn't make an error, beginning a streak of 47 errorless games for the man who is the best defensive shortstop in the history of the Cleveland franchise.

When Orel Hershiser signed with the Indians before the 1995 season, one of the first players he mentioned was Omar Vizquel. He talked about what a relief it would be to have Vizquel behind him at shortstop and how Vizquel is the best of the best at his position.

"Orel said that?" Vizquel asked. "I didn't even think he knew who I was."

Those listening to Vizquel smiled, but he wasn't kidding.

"With him being a great pitcher in the National League and me in the American League . . ." Vizquel's voice trailed off. "Well, I just didn't know he was paying attention. That makes my heart feel good — him talking like that about me."

When it comes to who catches the ball and who doesn't, pitchers pay very serious attention. And they know that the 28-year-old Vizquel catches almost everything.

All Hershiser had to do was watch ESPN and see the highlights of Chris Bosio's no-hitter against the Red Sox in 1993, when the final out for the Mariners came on a high-hopper over the mound. Vizquel dashed in, caught it with his bare hand and nipped Ernest Riles at first base with his throw.

"People asked how I could go for that ball with my bare hand," he said. "But how else can you make that play? I wanted that last ball hit to me to keep the no-hitter. I want every ball hit to me. I expect to make every play."

Vizquel pulled out his glove. It doesn't have a deep pocket "because I don't want the ball to get stuck in there when I go to throw it," he said.

Then he talked about his first baseball glove, the one under the Christmas tree when he was 5 years old. No, it wasn't gold. That would come later for the Indians shortstop.

"When he gave me the glove, my father told me that I had to take good care of it," Vizquel said. "He said it had to last for three years because he couldn't afford to buy me a new glove every year."

Vizquel took the glove to his bedroom and found a baseball in his closet.

"I put the ball in the glove, took a sock and tied it around the glove," he said.

That night, instead of hugging a teddy bear, Vizquel slept with his glove. And he did that for years.

"Sometimes I put my glove under my pillow," he said. "I kept it with me everywhere I went. In a couple of years, I found out that you can use baby oil on the glove, so I used to rub that into it. I loved my glove."

These days Vizquel can have as many gloves as he wants — free of charge. "But I only need one," he said.

True — you can only play with one glove at a time.

"I only use one glove all year," he said. "I break it in during spring training, and then use it all season."

Vizquel has three Rawlings gloves in his locker. Many players believe in switching from one glove to another during the course of a season. But he believes in one man, one glove — that's it. The other two are in his locker only as insurance, just in case something happens to his favorite.

"Some infielders use real small gloves, like their hands," he said. "But my glove is normal size. Nothing special."

No secrets to breaking it in? Does he use a special oil? A few squirts of tobacco juice in the pocket?

"Nothing," he said. "I don't put anything on it. I just catch balls with it. Lots of balls. That's how you get to be a good shortstop."

Then Vizquel said something rather strange.

"I don't really catch the ball," he said. "I just stop it with my glove. It stays up on top so I can switch it fast from my glove to my throwing hand."

This sounds like something you wouldn't want to try at home with your kid, but that is how this Picasso in spikes does it.

"But even I have my bad days," he said.

Yes. There was one bad day. It was April 16, 1994.

Vizquel booted two grounders and a pop-up. When most guys make three errors in a game, they throw out their glove to break the jinx. Vizquel tossed away his socks instead.

"I'd never give up my glove," he said. "It would never get that bad for me."

Despite that three-error game, Vizquel won a Gold Glove in 1994. It was his second. He won the first the previous year while playing for the Seattle Mariners.

But on that April 16, Vizquel's errors cost the Indians seven runs and the game. He stood before the media and accepted blame "for messing up the game. I apologize to my teammates and the fans."

Then he promised that he never would make three errors in a game again. To prove the point, he went two months and 56 more games before making even a single error.

Later it was learned that Vizquel had a fever and the flu on April 16, 1994. He was so sick that he couldn't even take infield practice, but he refused to use that as an excuse.

"This is a kid's game, but you have to be a man to play it," he said. "That is why I stood up. I hate excuses. But I never made three errors in a game, not even in Little League. That night, I called my father."

Omar Vizquel Sr. answered the phone in his apartment in Caracas, Venezuela. As he spoke, he could see his son's first Gold Glove award.

"It's right there, on the table," Vizquel said. "You can't miss it. The place is small, a two-bedroom apartment, the place where I grew up."

The elder Vizquel told his son not to worry. He told him he had excellent fundamentals. He told him to keep doing what he had always done: look the ball into his glove, take his time, plant his feet and make a good throw to first base.

"My father was the one who taught me how to play the position," Vizquel said. "My father hit me ground ball after ground ball. He'd watch me play and see the mistakes I made. He didn't push me; he just helped me."

Omar Vizquel Sr. had been a fine amateur shortstop in Venezuela.

"I've always wondered if he could have been a big-leaguer," Vizquel said. "But he came from a very poor family and had to go to work. He didn't have the chance that I had to try baseball."

Vizquel's father trained himself to be an electrician, enabling Omar Jr. to pick up a glove and follow his father's dream.

"I always was a shortstop, even when I was little," Vizquel said. "No one ever really coached me at the position but my father."

The elder Vizquel would take his son out to a nearby baseball diamond to practice his skills.

"The field was nothing but rocks and dirt," he said. "If you got a real bad hop back then, you could lose three teeth."

Vizquel was signed by the Mariners in 1984 and began his pro career at Class A Butte, Mont., in the Pioneer League. He moved up through the Mariners farm system and made his major league debut as the Mariners shortstop on opening day in 1989.

He was traded to the Indians on Dec. 20, 1993 in exchange for shortstop Felix Fermin and first baseman Reggie Jefferson.

Vizquel is a textbook middle infielder. He makes all of the routine plays and most of the spectacular ones. He doesn't seem to have a strong arm, but his throws invariably are chest-high, arriving at first base a step ahead of the runner.

"I do that to make the runner think he can beat it out," he said. "He may run like hell, but it's too late. The ball is always faster than the man."

He believes that there is a special relationship between the ball and the ballplayer.

"My father told me that you can either play with the ball, or it can play with you," he said. "If you watch me play catch, sometimes I flip the ball from my glove to my bare hand, or I catch the ball with the back of my glove. I do that to get a feel for the ball.

"Sometimes, I dribble the ball off my foot like a soccer player. I tell the soccer coaches back home that they should have their players practice with a baseball. That's harder to kick than a soccer ball."

Ask Mike Hargrove about Omar Vizquel and he'll say: "Catching ground balls shouldn't be that easy."

It isn't.

"It just looks that way," Vizquel said. "I've worked at it all my life. When I was little, we played a game called The Wall. I'd find another kid and a wall. We'd take a tennis ball and throw it against the wall, fielding grounders. The idea was to catch the ball fast and throw it past the other guy."

Vizquel played on concrete, on dirt, on clay, in a driveway, in a garage — "anywhere that there was a good wall, even in our apartment."

But his mother didn't like that idea, and she told him that baseball was meant to be played outside.

Vizquel will tell you that he can catch a ground ball almost anywhere.

"That's why I like grass fields instead of (artificial) turf," he said. "On turf, some guys look like great fielders. Then you see them on grass, and you find out that they really aren't so good."

Some had whispered that that would happen to Vizquel when the Indians traded for him in December of 1993. He was the top American League shortstop in Seattle's Kingdome, where all the hops were quick and true. But grass and dirt can play tricks with the ball, especially in the infields in northern climates.

"I love playing here, on this team," Vizquel said. "At Jacobs Field, the infield is like a carpet. I get more attention from the fans and writers. I think it helps more people know about me."

Vizquel is a proud man from Caracas, and he talks about the line of Venezuelan shortstops — Luis Aparicio, Chico Carrasquel, Dave Concepcion, Ozzie Guillen and himself.

"To me, the greatest honor is to be compared to Aparicio," he said. "I never saw him play, but people back home still talk about him."

Now they follow Vizquel in the Caracas newspapers, which carry weekly reports on the Venezuelan players in the major leagues. In 1994, there was an Omar Vizquel calendar on sale in Venezuela; it featured a picture of Omar for every month of the year. He is a hero at home, where it means the most.

"My friends, they keep me humble," Vizquel said. "When I don't hit much for a few games, I get letters from people at home wanting to know what is wrong with me. I tell them, 'Hey, I feel bad, too. I want to be a part of the hitting machine we have here in Cleveland.' And when I make an error, they really let me hear it."

Vizquel is one of the most approachable and affable players in the Tribe clubhouse. In an informal poll of those scribes who cover the team, Vizquel was picked as their favorite player. Why? Because he is so professional on the field and so downright decent when you talk to him.

And to Vizquel, knowing that he is appreciated for his personality and classy conduct is the best compliment of all.

10

THE QUALITY OF LEADERSHIP

June 30, 1995: Eddie Murray slapped a single between the first and second basemen. It was Murray's 3,000th hit. It was in the sixth inning of a game against the Twins in the Metrodome. The Indians went on to beat Minnesota, 4-1. The Indians raised their record to 41-17, nine games ahead of the second-place Kansas City Royals, and it wasn't even July yet. The winning pitcher in the game was Dennis Martinez. That was appropriate because Martinez and Murray both started their big-league careers in the same year (1977) and in the same place (Baltimore). They even signed to play with the Indians on the same date — Dec. 2, 1993.

The first time I saw Eddie Murray was in the spring of 1979. He was a 23-year-old first baseman for the Baltimore Orioles. I was a 23-year-old rookie baseball writer for the Baltimore Evening Sun.

Earl Weaver was the Orioles manager, and he was telling me about Murray.

"If Eddie would listen to me, he'd make millions," Weaver said.

I was confused and waited for Weaver to explain. In 1978, Murray had batted .285 with 27 homers and 95 RBI and was named to the All-Star team — all before his 23rd birthday. Tribe fans would never believe it based on how he has played first base for Cleveland, but a younger, more flexible Murray won three Gold Gloves at that position for the Orioles.

And Weaver was telling me he wanted to turn Murray into a catcher?

"Name one switch-hitting catcher who was worth a damn," Weaver said.

I couldn't think of any.

"Look at that," Weaver said, pointing to Murray. The Orioles were practicing their bunt defense. Murray roared in from first base, picked up a slow roller with his bare hand, and, all in one motion, unleashed a missile to third base to force out a runner.

"He's got a cannon for an arm," Weaver said. "He's got good size (6-foot-2, 220 pounds), and he's smart. He'd hit a ton. I'm telling you, he'd break the bank if he were a catcher."

Weaver believed the formula to winning was pitching and three-run homers. He was convinced he could find another power hitter to play first if Murray would go behind the plate.

In 1979, Weaver's catcher was Rick Dempsey. Weaver loved Dempsey's arm and his grit, because Dempsey would block the plate on any base runner. But the bat turned to balsa in Dempsey's hands. While Dempsey fostered an image as a thinking-man's catcher, Weaver and a number of players called him "Rock Head" when he was with the Orioles. Dempsey was stubborn and not exactly a Jim Hegan or even a Tony Pena when it came to calling a game. Orioles pitchers were free to shake off Dempsey and follow their own instincts.

Did Weaver want to run Dempsey out of town? No way. Was he always thinking about getting a catcher who could hit homers? You bet.

In the spring of 1979, the big money had just begun to dribble into baseball. A guy making $250,000 was considered one of the best-paid players in the leagues. Murray was earning less than $100,000.

So Weaver was appealing to Murray's bank account when he made his pitch for switching to catcher.

"Does Eddie want to catch?" I asked Weaver.

"No," Weaver said. "At least not yet."

When Murray began playing for the Indians in 1994, I reminded him of Weaver's plans.

"He talked about that a lot," Murray said. "But I'd tell him, 'Earl, I'm going to make millions of dollars anyway. What do I want to catch for? I want to play this game a long time.' Even when I was in the minors, they wanted to make me into a catcher. They kept telling me that I had a great arm and I'd get to the big leagues faster. I was only 18 when I signed. I told them that I had plenty of time. I'd get there on my own."

And that is exactly what Murray did.

To know Eddie Murray, you must understand two things: his life with his family in Los Angeles and his days with the Baltimore Orioles.

Murray was one of 12 children born to Charles and Carrie Murray. Charles spent 30 years at the Ludlow Rug Co. as a mechanic. Carrie was busy with the kids.

East L.A. in the 1960s was not the war zone that it is today, but it wasn't quaint Medina, Ohio, either. The Murrays wanted to keep their kids out of trouble, and that meant keeping them busy and keeping them close to home. It meant sports and family.

In their backyard, the Murray boys would play games of baseball. A telephone pole was first base, a hole in the ground was second, a clothesline pole was third and home plate was a slab of cement. Sometimes they used rubber balls or tennis balls. When they ran out of balls, they used the plastic lids from Crisco cans.

"Man, you could throw a wicked curve with those things," Murray recalled.

One time, the Murray boys went too far. They took the heads off their sisters' dolls and used them for baseballs. Carrie Murray told her sons that if they ever did that again, well, they would never play baseball again.

To the Murray boys, that would have been death. Baseball was life. It was their oxygen. They played day and night. They took turns playing different positions. They made up teams — one of the boys usually took the Dodgers, the other the Giants. They made out lineups from those rosters, and, as they batted, they had to imitate the stance of the different players.

That meant batting right-handed and left-handed. It was how Murray became a switch-hitter, but he didn't know it at the time.

Eddie Murray will tell you that he wasn't the best ballplayer in the family. The oldest brother, Charles, was best. He hammered 37 homers and drove in 119 runs for Class A Modesto back in 1964. But Vietnam was hotter than Charles Murray's bat, and his career was torpedoed by two stints in the military. He leveled out at Class AAA and then went to work as a prison guard.

Eddie's next-oldest brother, Leon, was an outfielder who played a year of pro ball and then blew out his shoulder and was released. Leon Murray was very good with scissors and served as the family barber. When Eddie played for Baltimore, he sometimes took his teammates to his house when the Orioles were in Los Angeles. Leon would cut the players' hair, and Murray's mother would barbecue ribs.

A third Murray brother, Venice, played a year of pro ball and then saw his career shattered by a major injury to his knee.

The youngest brother, Rich, was the only other Murray to make the majors. A first baseman like Eddie, Rich couldn't stick in the big leagues for long. Willie McCovey said that Rich Murray was the man to replace him at first base with the Giants, but Rich batted only 204 times and hit just .216 for San Francisco. The Indians had Rich Murray in their training camp in the spring of 1981. Former team president Gabe Paul spent $20,000 to draft Murray from the Giants, explaining, "I know that he hasn't done that much yet, but I like his genes." Well, some scouting reports are better than others, and Rich Murray didn't last with the Tribe. But he later served as a coach in the Indians' minor league system during the 1994 season.

Those are four Murray brothers. Eddie is the fifth.

The Orioles made Eddie Murray their third-round pick in the summer of 1973. He was only 17, but he had already graduated from high school. When a Baltimore scout visited the Murray home, he found Eddie to be shy and withdrawn. Heck, he was 17. Why wouldn't he be scared?

But Murray's three older brothers had played pro ball. They had some very strong opinions about Eddie's worth, and they worried that Eddie would be tossed aside after a year if he were injured. After all, that was the experience of Venice and Leon.

Exactly what happened when the Orioles were trying to sign Murray is a sore spot with Eddie.

During the 1979 World Series, when Murray's Orioles were playing the Pirates, New York sportswriter Dick Young wrote a story about the scout's visit to the Murray home. Young quoted the scout as saying that Murray's brothers had belligerent attitudes and were bitter about their minor league experiences. The story implied that there was some racism — that the brothers didn't trust the scout because he was white. The Murray brothers allegedly yelled at him and threw him out of the house.

Eddie Murray says that isn't what happened, although he won't discuss it in detail. Parts of the story were exaggerated and other parts were downright lies, according to Murray. The scout later said that Young had taken some quotes "out of context."

This story became Murray's first brush fire with the media. He was livid with Young, because Young never asked him for his version. He also believed that the story wasn't just an attack on him, but on his entire family. And nothing in the world meant more to Murray than his family.

The whole thing was a mess, a wound that festered in Murray's heart.

After the story appeared, Murray went 1-for-21 in the rest of the 1979 World Series. Weaver will tell you that the story was the reason. Murray, then only 23, was so upset and hurt that he just lost his concentration.

The Orioles, of course, did sign Murray, and they sent him to Bluefield, W.Va. Talk about culture shock. You take a black kid from urban Los Angeles and drop him in the middle of the Blue Ridge Mountains before his 18th birthday. It was exactly the kind of thing the Murray brothers were worried about. They knew Eddie was young and needed time and patience to find himself. They also knew what a grind a player has to endure in the low minors.

But like most everything else that later would come Murray's way, if Bluefield did bother him, Eddie refused to show it.

In 50 games, he ripped 11 homers and hit .287. At this time, he was strictly a right-handed-hitting first baseman.

During this summer when Murray was still 17, he was one of 1,000 minor league baseball players who were given a battery of psychological tests. These tests don't always predict greatness, but they were prophetic in Murray's case. He scored in the 93rd percentile in the category of "drive and desire to succeed."

In the category of "emotional control," Murray finished in the 99th percentile. To him, that was no surprise. His mother continually had told him, "Eddie, if you can't control yourself, then what can you control?"

Ever notice how Murray shows the same face to the world, no matter whether he strikes out or hits a home run? He has a Barry White, a Walt Frazier, a Jim Brown kind of cool. You don't talk trash. You don't show up your opponent and you don't throw your bat and make a scene when your opponent gets the best of you.

Ever notice how he talks about baseball being a game that is played one pitch, one at-bat, and one inning at a time? Well, a lot of guys say that, but Murray believes it.

Murray didn't become a switch-hitter until late in the 1975 season. He was playing for Asheville in the Class AA Southern League. One day, Manager Jimmy Schaffer walked by the batting cage. Schaffer heard the crack of the bat — a sound like lightning splitting a tree. He squinted into the North Carolina sun and noticed that Murray was hitting left-handed. He realized that bolt had come off Murray's bat.

"Can you really hit left-handed?" Schaffer asked.

"Yeah, I can," Murray said.

"Good, keep working on it," Schaffer replied.

Murray did. It was no big deal. He felt as if he were batting in the backyard against his brothers, imitating the stances of the entire Dodgers lineup from the late 1960s. He finished that 1975 season hitting 10-for-31 left-handed, and he has been a switch-hitter ever since. And that switch-hitting put him on the fast track to Baltimore.

"I'd never even heard of Eddie until the winter (of 1976-77)," Earl Weaver recalled. "I started getting reports on this kid Murray, who was having a great year down in Puerto Rico. The scouts said that it might be worth giving him a look in spring training."

When the Orioles assembled in Miami in February of 1977, Murray was only 21. He had played only 54 games in Class AAA. The idea was to give him a taste of the majors and then send him to Class AAA Rochester for seasoning.

"We never believed in rushing our players," Weaver said. "We had a good team with a lot of depth. We believed it was better to bring a guy up a year late rather than bring him up a year early."

The idea was that no player was ever destroyed by extra exposure to the minors — it just gave him more experience and confidence. But coming to the big leagues too young and too soon — that has ruined too many careers.

"Another thing was that back in 1977, we had Lee May as our first baseman," Weaver said. "He was in the prime of his career (hitting 25 homers and leading the American League with 109 RBI in 1976). I wasn't in the market for another first baseman."

But Weaver did want another bat.

"Reggie Jackson had been our designated hitter, but he went free agent (signing with the New York Yankees)," Weaver said. "I gave Eddie a chance to play in our two intrasquad games, and he hit a lot of rockets. Then he played in our first few exhibition games, and he hit one ball off the 420-foot wall in center. That night, we had a staff meeting to make our first cuts. Everyone in the room wanted to send Eddie to the minor league camp. I told (General Manager) Hank Peters: 'We can't do that, it would wreck the kid's morale. He hasn't done a thing wrong yet. Let's wait a week.' So we waited a week; Eddie kept hitting, but the staff wanted to send him out anyway. I said, 'Give the kid another week.' It went like that all spring."

In their final meeting to pick the roster, Peters asked Weaver: "Earl, I know Eddie has been great, but where are you going to play him? We can't let a kid like this just sit on the bench."

"Hank, I'll play him," Weaver said. "I'll find a spot for him as long as he hits."

Murray opened the 1977 season as the Orioles designated hitter. He was a better defensive first baseman than Lee May, but Weaver was not about to take the position away from May and give it to a rookie. Weaver's Orioles didn't treat their veterans like that.

Nor did veterans tolerate much from young players. When Murray would express an opinion about something, May would yell: "Shut up, rookie, you ain't done nothing yet up here."

By midseason, Weaver had used Murray a little at third base and in the outfield, but he was still primarily a DH. The manager also was trying to convince Murray to catch. Meanwhile, May became Murray's mentor, and the two men would sit in a corner of the dressing room — May explaining the facts of big-league life and Murray nodding, soaking it up, asking questions.

"I'll never forget how Lee treated me," Murray said. "When I came to the Orioles, he wasn't ready to give up his position. Instead, he and his family did everything they could to help me. He showed me how things were done with the Orioles."

May was one of the most respected members of the team, and he really did believe that the team came first. When May would hear pitcher Jim Palmer popping off to a writer about how he was underpaid and how the Orioles should renegotiate his contract, May would yell across the the dressing room: "Hey, Palmer, where was the gun?"

"What gun?" asked Palmer.

"The gun they put to your head to make you sign that contract," May said.

Then May and the other players would laugh. It would embarrass Palmer into silence. May knew that Palmer's obsession with money and forever wanting a new contract wasn't healthy for the team, so he wanted to stop the dialogue right there.

May was more than a barrel-chested guy who hit a lot of homers; he was the manager's best friend. May knew that he was The Past and Murray was The Future. If May had wanted to make Murray's life miserable, he could have done so because other players would have followed his lead. Instead of sulking about the young rookie, he began to train the man who would take his job.

Murray was the American League's 1977 Rookie of the Year. By 1978, he had become the Orioles' starting first baseman and he made his first All-Star team. May, in the meantime, had moved to DH.

Weaver was pleased to see the relationship growing between Murray and May. To Weaver, May was the ultimate professional — a quiet, no-nonsense guy.

Weaver tells this story of what could have been one of his roughest days as a manager. It was late in May's career, and the right-handed batter had seen his skills erode to the extent that he could not hit a right-handed pitcher with a decent curveball. But that was the situation late in a close game. May was in the on-deck circle, and Weaver called May back into the dugout.

He couldn't look May in the eye. He sent lefty Dan Graham to bat for him. Then Weaver walked into the dugout runway to smoke a cigarette — his habit when the Orioles were in a tough spot. He also didn't want to see May. From a baseball standpoint, Weaver knew he had made the right move. But he thought of all that May had done for the Orioles and of how May was such a proud and dignified man. In a perfect world, no one should ever pinch-hit for Lee May.

Weaver was thinking all this when Baltimore pitching coach Ray Miller said, "Earl, take a look down in the bullpen."

Weaver stuck his head out of the dugout and saw May warming up a relief pitcher, because May knew that was what Graham had been doing before he was sent in to pinch-hit. Weaver smiled. No manager could ask for more support than that. May could have pouted at the end of the bench. He could have kicked the water cooler. He could have cussed out the manager for sending a nobody like Dan Graham to bat for him. And if May had done any or all of those things, Weaver would not have blamed him.

Instead, May put the team first. Young players such as Murray saw that. No one said a word. Nothing needed to be said.

These were the Orioles, a team that finished in either first or second place in 15 of 18 seasons from 1966 to 1983. This was where Eddie Murray learned his baseball.

A lot happened between the time when Eddie Murray was a young player with the Orioles in the late 1970s and the day when Eddie Murray signed to play for the Indians in 1994.

Murray had never been Mr. Sunshine when it came to the media. Neither had Lee May, for that matter. But players in general view the notebook and the microphone set with suspicion. Though they don't think that every sportswriter is out to stir up trouble, they believe that's a safe general rule under which to operate.

Murray can give you the kind of look that would crumble Mount Rushmore. Ask him a question, and he seldom answers immediately. You might think he is glaring at you, but he's really trying to size you up. He likes to think before he answers, and often the best way to get him to talk is to keep your mouth shut and listen. Present a question and then wait, even if the silence seems forbidding and uncomfortable, and Murray often will give an answer full of insight.

He played for the Orioles from 1977 to 1988, leaving as the team's all-time home-run leader (333) and in second place in RBI (1,190). He played the next three years with the Los Angeles Dodgers, then moved on to the New York Mets for two years.

The scribes who covered the Mets were, for the most part, New Yorkers. Culturally, there is something about those who are raised in The City That Never Sleeps that forces them to talk incessantly and to talk loud — traits that didn't appeal to Murray.

"I don't know if the media in Cleveland could act like the guys in New York, even if they wanted to," Murray has often said.

He went to war with the New York media during his first week of spring training. Some New York players had been accused of sexual assault by a woman in Florida. A New York newspaper carried the story in huge headlines, and next to that story was a picture of Murray refusing to sign an autograph.

Murray was not one of the accused players. He has never been in trouble with the law or with management. Twice he has been nominated for the prestigious Roberto Clemente Award for his charitable work on behalf of the Red Cross, Johns Hopkins Children's Center, United Cerebral Palsy and other humanitarian organizations. Those who know Murray will attest to the fact that he has raised millions of dollars for good causes.

To Murray, his picture next to the story — even though the story didn't mention him — implicated him in the unsavory activity and undercut everything he had done to be a good citizen.

"After that, everything went downhill with the media in New York," Murray said. "My two years there felt like five. In New York, the media doesn't want you to do well."

The New York media lashed back. They said Murray was a cancer in the clubhouse. They said he was selfish. When he played first base, Murray had a habit of folding his arms across his chest and looking absolutely bored between pitches, as if he'd rather be anywhere else. The media charged him with not always running hard on routine outs and said he was a bad example to the younger players.

In his two years with the Mets, Murray averaged 22 homers and 96 RBI. When he became a free agent after the 1993 season, he wasn't sure where he would sign — he just knew that it would not be in New York.

Meanwhile, Indians General Manager John Hart was shopping for a designated hitter to bat fifth, behind Albert Belle. The Candy Maldonado Era was over. In 1993, Maldonado, Paul Sorrento, and others had tried the spot, and opposing pitchers discovered they would rather face Sorrento or anyone else on the Tribe roster than Belle. So they began to "work around Belle," meaning they would pitch out of the strike zone. If Belle wanted to chase those pitches, fine. If not, he could just walk to first base and the pitcher would take his chances with whomever was up next.

Sometimes, Belle walked. Other times, he swung at terrible pitches and made outs. Either way, he was growing more frustrated by the day.

"The guy who bats behind Albert has to have a reputation," Hart said. "He also has to be used to handling pressure. It took a special person."

When Murray became available, Hart heard all the horror stories from New York. He didn't buy them.

"I came up in the Orioles organization as a minor league manager and a coach," Hart said. "I knew Eddie and what he meant to a team."

He also knew that even at 37, Murray could still hit.

Murray has a career batting average of .416 with the bases loaded. He has never driven in fewer than 75 runs in any season — or fewer than 84 in a season when no games were lost to strikes.

Only twice in his long career has Murray been on the disabled list, and only Cincinnati's Pete Rose has more seasons of appearing in 150 games than Murray.

Guess who Cal Ripken named as his role model for playing every day.

"It was Eddie who taught me consistency and how to prepare yourself," Ripken said. "I learned more baseball from him than anyone else I've played with."

That was the Eddie Murray that John Hart knew, and that was the Eddie Murray who signed with the Indians before the 1994 season.

It was a perfect match. With the Indians, Murray was happy to play his game and let the media put the spotlight on young stars such as Carlos

Baerga, Kenny Lofton and Belle. He was happy that Dennis Martinez never met a reporter he didn't like, and Martinez was willing to talk to people about Murray.

Eddie Murray could just hit, and hit he did. Despite playing with a sprained right thumb for much of 1994, he batted .254 with 17 homers and 76 RBI in 108 games. More important, he hit .331 with runners in scoring position, taking the heat off Belle.

In 1995, Murray kept hitting. And he was making baseball history. There was the 3,000th hit. There is the quest for 500 career homers; he is only 21 short. This was a man bearing down on 40, yet he hit .323 with 21 homers and 82 RBI. The numbers would have been even bigger had he not broken two ribs in his left side on July 2, two days after his 3,000th hit. Murray was out for a month because he slid into home plate, colliding with Minnesota catcher Matt Walbeck.

Manager Mike Hargrove appreciates Murray's production, but he also relishes the veteran's attitude.

"Eddie is not afraid to get on a guy if he makes a mistake," Hargrove said. "Some players are more willing to listen to Eddie Murray than to a manager or coach, so Eddie makes my job easier. We have a number of leaders on this team, but Eddie is at the head of the pack."

It is easy for a veteran player to put his arm around a guy and say, "Don't worry, everything is going to be all right." It is much harder to get in the player's face and say, "Get your act together; you'll screw up the whole team if you don't pull your head out of your butt."

"Eddie got that from Lee May," said Frank Robinson, a long-time Orioles player, coach, manager and executive. "With the Orioles, we weren't afraid to confront each other. I did it when I played. Lee May did it. Eddie did it. I'm sure he is like that in Cleveland. Now, some people resent that. But, hey, you can't be liked all the time. Guys don't always need a pat in the back. Sometimes they need a kick in the ass."

Murray agrees.

"Some of today's players will take the challenge when you talk to them; others will lay down," he said. "But you can't let little things go by. The little things in this game are what beat you and what can keep a good team from being even better. You can't have guys missing the cutoff man and throwing the ball all over the park. You can't have guys who refuse to pay attention. If I see that, then I'll speak up."

Fortunately for Tribe fans, the players usually listened.

11

When You've Got The Gift

July 16, 1995: When Manny Ramirez hit the ball, all Dennis Eckersley could do was stand and say, "Wow!" Eckersley threw the pitch that Manny hit and that ball went about 400 feet into the left-field bleachers. The hit cost Eckersley and his Oakland A's the game. An hour after the Indians had won yet again — this time in the bottom of the 12th inning — all Eckersley could talk about was Ramirez. "Wow," repeated Eckersley for the millionth time. "Most young guys in that situation would be just trying to make contact and get a base hit, but he goes long. I mean, he went right out of his shoes on that pitch." Ramirez's slam turned what would have been a 4-3 loss into a 5-4 victory. The Indians' record was 50-21, 14 games ahead of the second-place Kansas City Royals.

Some people have a gift. For whatever reason, the Almighty ordained Jesse Owens to run . . . Nat King Cole (and his daughter) to sing . . . Fred Astaire to dance . . . James Earl Jones to speak with a voice that sounds as if it came from God himself.

And, yes, Manny Ramirez was born to hit.

All of these people owe their success to natural talent, but talent isn't everything.

James Earl Jones had a voice made for radio, but he became a stage and screen star. He did it with desire and work. He was born with a severe stuttering problem, and he took special education classes and forced himself to speak in front of groups to overcome his stuttering. He did it because he knew that The Gift wasn't enough. The Gift was a privilege and he was obligated to make the most of it.

That remains the challenge facing Manny Ramirez.

Can he hit?

Could Martin Luther King preach? Could John Steinbeck write?

The Gift is there. It is Ramirez's blessing, but every blessing carries a responsibility.

Sometimes, having The Gift makes a person think that he needs nothing else — that the world should genuflect at the mere mention of his name. So hot rock stars ask for a bowl of M&Ms before a show and demand that there be no red or green ones in the bowl. Movie stars and superstar jocks break contracts, scorn their fans, and pretend that the rules of civil behavior apply only to Someone Else.

The Gift can lead to excess. It can turn good people bad. It can make weak people easy targets for those who soothe their egos with one hand and steal their wallets with the other.

The Gift brought Manny Ramirez to the big leagues. It enabled him to beat astounding odds to become perhaps the best young hitter in today's game, the kind of guy who may one day win the Triple Crown.

When Indians scout Joe DeLucca first spotted Ramirez at New York's George Washington High, he made this report: "He's a hitting machine."

Other Indians scouts came to see this babe of the bat. They compared him to Hank Aaron, to Roberto Clemente, to Ted Williams. They tried to control themselves but couldn't.

Ramirez may have been 18, painfully shy, and educationally deprived, but he was a virtuoso with the bat.

The Indians discovered in 1991 what Ramirez's friends and family had known for years: Manny was special. The problem was that Manny knew it, too. Because Manny always could hit, he felt no need to learn English. He has been in this country since the age of 13, yet his hold on the English language is far more tenuous than that of many of his Latin teammates who haven't been here nearly as long.

Some point to the fact that Ramirez never bothered to graduate from high school and say, "Hey, he's dumb as a stone. No wonder he can't learn English."

Not true.

There is nothing wrong with Manny's natural intellect. He didn't work hard in school because he saw no reason for it. He had The Gift. He could hit. His identity was based upon the sound of his bat, not his voice.

Consider this story: During his first year as a pro, the 19-year-old Ramirez was playing at Class A Burlington, N.C. He was three hours late for treatment of a bruised thigh.

"Manny, what happened?" asked Dave Keller, his manager.

"I don't know," Ramirez said.

"Why were you late?" Keller asked again.

"I don't know," Ramirez mumbled.

That is the same answer he often gives to reporters and fans.

"Manny, what happened when you were picked off?" they would ask.

"I don't know," he'd say.

"How about when you missed the cutoff man?"

"I don't know," he'd shrug.

Ramirez would have to be a complete dunderhead not to know the answer to some of those questions. Believe me, Manny does know. But because he has The Gift and because his gift is hitting in a culture in which baseball is treated with religious reverence, well, Manny has not had to answer for much. He could let his bat do the talking.

From the moment he signed with the Indians, the orders from the front office were, "Don't anyone touch Manny's swing."

But his coaches and managers also were told: "We've got to help this kid grow up, and grow up fast."

The Indians realize that having The Gift isn't enough. Ramirez's long-term success ultimately will be dictated by whether he knows what to do when he doesn't have a bat in his hands. In the meantime, he struggles. He is better this year than he was a year ago. He should have a firmer grasp on life by next year.

But there are frustrations, for both Ramirez and the Indians. In spring training, the Tribe began trying to work out a long term contract with Ramirez, and the process continued through the 1995 season. A couple of times, they thought they were close, but Ramirez kept changing agents. He went through three of them in 1995, and has had at least five during his brief pro career. Even Manny may have lost count of them.

There is a story about Ramirez in a video store. He wanted to rent some movies, but when he tried to check them out, it was discovered that he owed more than $200 for movies he rented but forgot to return.

What the Indians keep trying to tell Ramirez is this: You have to keep track of more than your batting average, be it your money or even your rented movies.

Ramirez and his parents are from Santiago, a large city in the Dominican Republic. His parents are hard-working people who discovered that their sweat led to nothing but tears in their native land. They heard about the United States, especially New York, where so many Dominicans have moved and made a life for themselves — a life with running water and decent medical care, a life where a man could start his own business without having to pay huge bribes to the police or criminals.

Aristides and Onlecidad Ramirez brought their family to New York in 1985. Aristides went to work as a cab driver; Onlecidad became a seamstress in the garment district. They lived in Washington which is on the northern edge of Manhattan. Their apartment was on 168th Street. There were three bedrooms and no telephone for Manny, his parents and his four older sisters. Yes, this was New York, but life still was much closer to the Dominican Republic than to Park Avenue. Spanish was the language, salsa music was the soundtrack, and rice and beans the favorite food.

When people moved from the Dominican Republic to New York, it didn't take them long to discover that the streets weren't paved with gold, but they still believed that this was a special country. For all its faults, New York was better than home. Think about it. How often do you hear about someone from the United States wanting to move back to the Dominican Republic?

Manny Ramirez first displayed The Gift of baseball in the Dominican Republic, but it was at George Washington High where he became a neighborhood legend.

He hit so much that even the stuffy New York Times took notice. During his senior year, the Times did an eight-part series on Ramirez and his team. The paper made Manny its adopted son and continued to run lengthy stories on him every few months.

Imagine being 18 and being Manny Ramirez. You may not be able to read the story, but you see your face in the New York Times. Your friends and relatives tell you that this is important, that the Times is the greatest newspaper of them all and seldom do they write about anyone from the Dominican community. If you are in the New York Times, you are special.

If you were a young Manny Ramirez, would you spend a lot of time with the books? Would you listen when people told you that learning English was critical to your future? Would you think about anything but baseball?

And Manny did indeed care about baseball. He knew that he had to get stronger, and he'd wake at 6 most mornings to push his body. His favorite exercise involved working with an old tire and a rope. He would tie the rope around his waist and connect it to the tire. Then he would run at least a mile through the streets and alleys of New York, dragging that tire

Matt Detrich

A sellout crowd was the norm at Jacobs Field in 1995 as the Cleveland Indians became a championship team for the first time in 41 years. The opening of the new ballpark in 1994 coincided with the team's resurgence as an American League powerhouse.

Manny Ramirez takes off for first after hitting a single in a game against Milwaukee. The 23-year-old Ramirez batted .308 in 1995 with 31 home runs and 107 RBI.

Mike Cardew

All photos by Akron Beacon Journal staff members.

Mike Cardew

Indians closer Jose Mesa fires a pitch during a game against Detroit. Mesa saved a team-record 46 games in 1995 and set a major league record with 38 consecutive saves.

Centerfielder Kenny Lofton is beseiged by fans seeking an autograph before the start of a game at Jacobs Field.

Mike Cardew

Mike Cardew

Albert Belle hammers a home run in a game against the Milwaukee Brewers. In 1995 Belle became the first player in major league history to hit 50 homers and 50 doubles in the same season.

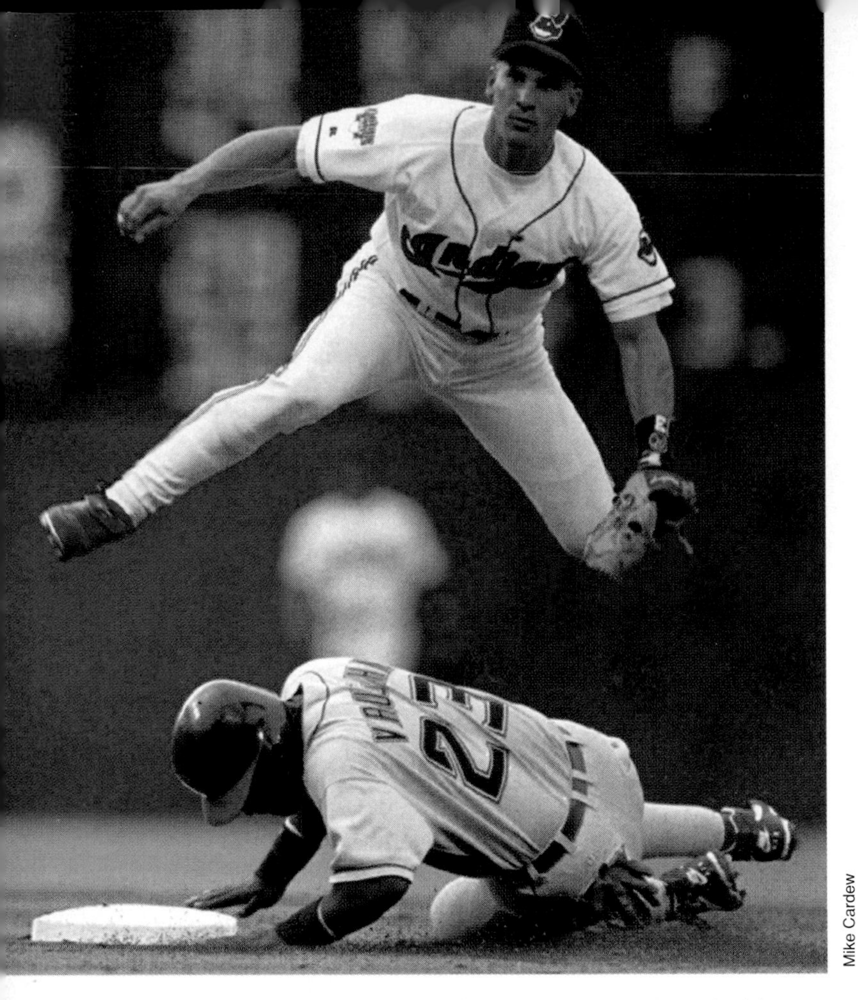

Mike Cardew

Leaping above Milwaukee Brewer Greg Vaughn to make a double play, Omar Vizquel displays the form that made him the only Indians shortstop to win a Gold Glove award for outstanding fielding.

Fans Jim Ellsworth of Parma and Brett Connors of Cleveland celebrate as the Indians secure their 100th win by beating the Kansas City Royals at Jacobs Field in the final game of the season on Oct. 1.

Matt Detrich

Matt Detrich

Jose Mesa raises his fist in victory after the Indians clinch the Central Division title at Jacobs Field on Sept. 8. The Indians went on to win their division by a record 30 games.

Pitcher Dennis Martinez started Game 1 of the first round of the American League playoffs at Jacobs Field. Martinez, a 1995 All-Star with a 12-5 record for the season, pitched six innings of the rain-delayed, 13-inning game.

Mike Cardew

Catcher Tony Pena gets a hug from Orel Hershiser after hitting a home run in Game 1 of the playoffs. At 2:08 a.m. with two outs in the bottom of the 13th inning, Pena swung at a 3-0 pitch and sent the ball into the left-field bleachers. Pena's homer gave the Indians a 5-4 victory over the Boston Red Sox.

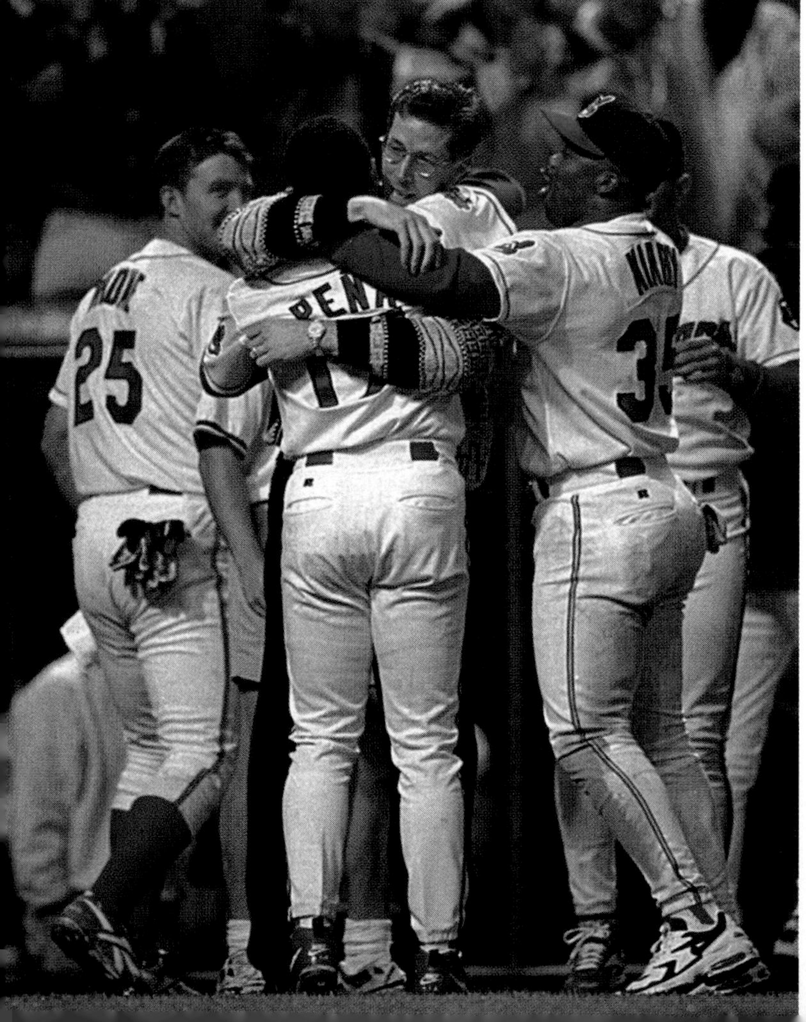

Phil Masturzo

Mike Cardew

Eddie Murray rounds second after hitting a triple in Game 2 of the first playoff round against the Boston Red Sox. Murray, who got his 3,000th hit during the 1995 season, also homered in the game, which the Indians won, 4-0.

Phil Masturzo

Phil Masturzo

Omar Vizquel robs Seattle Mariner Jay Buhner of a hit in Game 2 of the American League Championship Series.

Orel Hershiser sets up for a pitch in the first inning of Game 2 against Seattle. He allowed just one run on four hits in eight innings. The Indians won the game, 5-2, and tied the best-of-seven series at one game apiece.

Phil Masturzo

His hitting and base-running made Kenny Lofton one of the Indians' most valuable players in the American League Championship Series. In the photo above, Lofton watches his fifth-inning hit that drove in Alvaro Espinoza for the first run in Game 6. In the eighth inning of that same game, Lofton scored from second base after a fastball got away from Mariners catcher Dan Wilson and rolled to the Tribe dugout. In the photo below, Lofton slides safely past Mike Blowers into third base after hitting a triple in the third inning of Game 3. Lofton also stole a base and singled in that game.

Ed Suba Jr.

Rocky Colavito rears back to throw out the first pitch at Jacobs Field to start Game 5 of the American League Championship Series. While the trade of the former Indians star to Detroit in 1960 signaled the start of more than three decades of misery for Tribe fans, his presence on this night brought nothing but luck. Despite making four errors, the Indians were able to beat the Mariners, 3-2.

Ed Suba Jr.

Jim Thome celebrates his two-run homer in the sixth inning of Game 5 with teammates Omar Vizquel and Wayne Kirby.

Phil Masturzo

Phil Masturzo

Dennis Martinez prepares to fire one across the plate during Game 6 of the American League Championship Series. Martinez pitched seven innings, giving up only four hits. The 4-0 Cleveland victory was Martinez's first post-season win of his career.

The Indians celebrate on the field after beating Seattle in Game 6 and bringing Cleveland the American League pennant for the first time in 41 years.

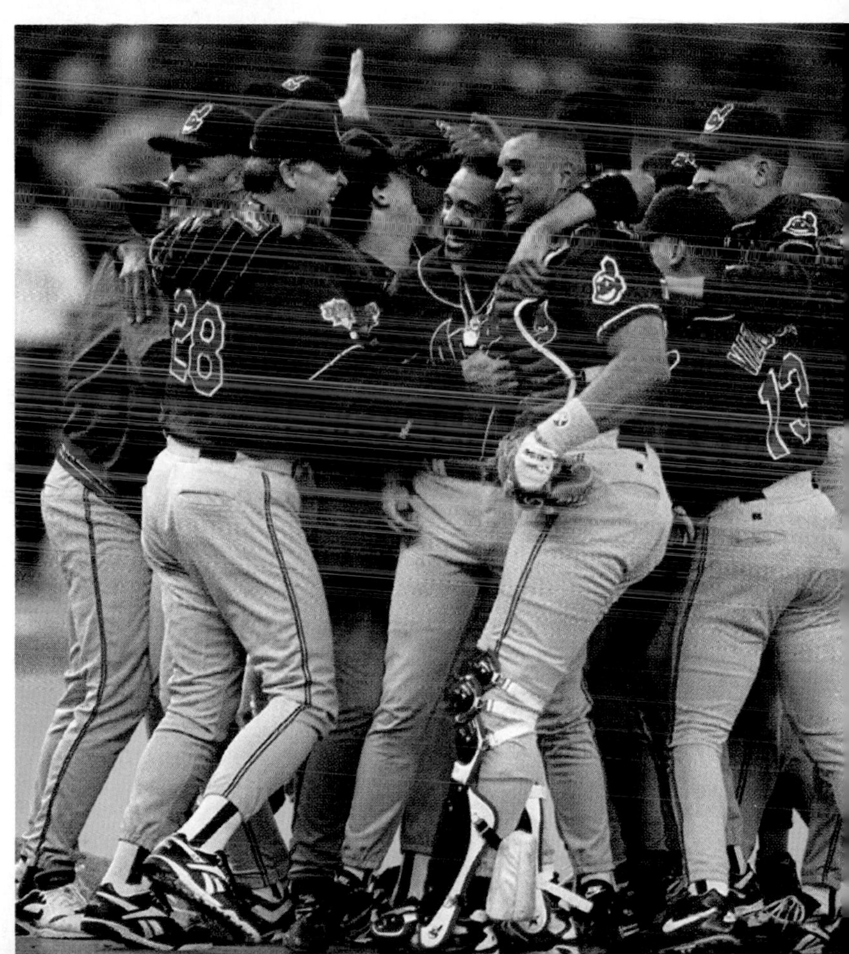

Ed Suba Jr.

Charles Nagy was Cleveland's starting pitcher in Game 3 of the World Series. The Indians got their first victory over the Braves in the game, beating Atlanta, 7-6, in 11 innings.

Phil Masturzo

Alvaro Espinoza gets a hug from Jim Thome after scoring the winning run on an Eddie Murray single in the 11th inning of Game 3 of the World Series. Sandy Alomar and Carlos Baerga run to meet them.

Ed Suba Jr.

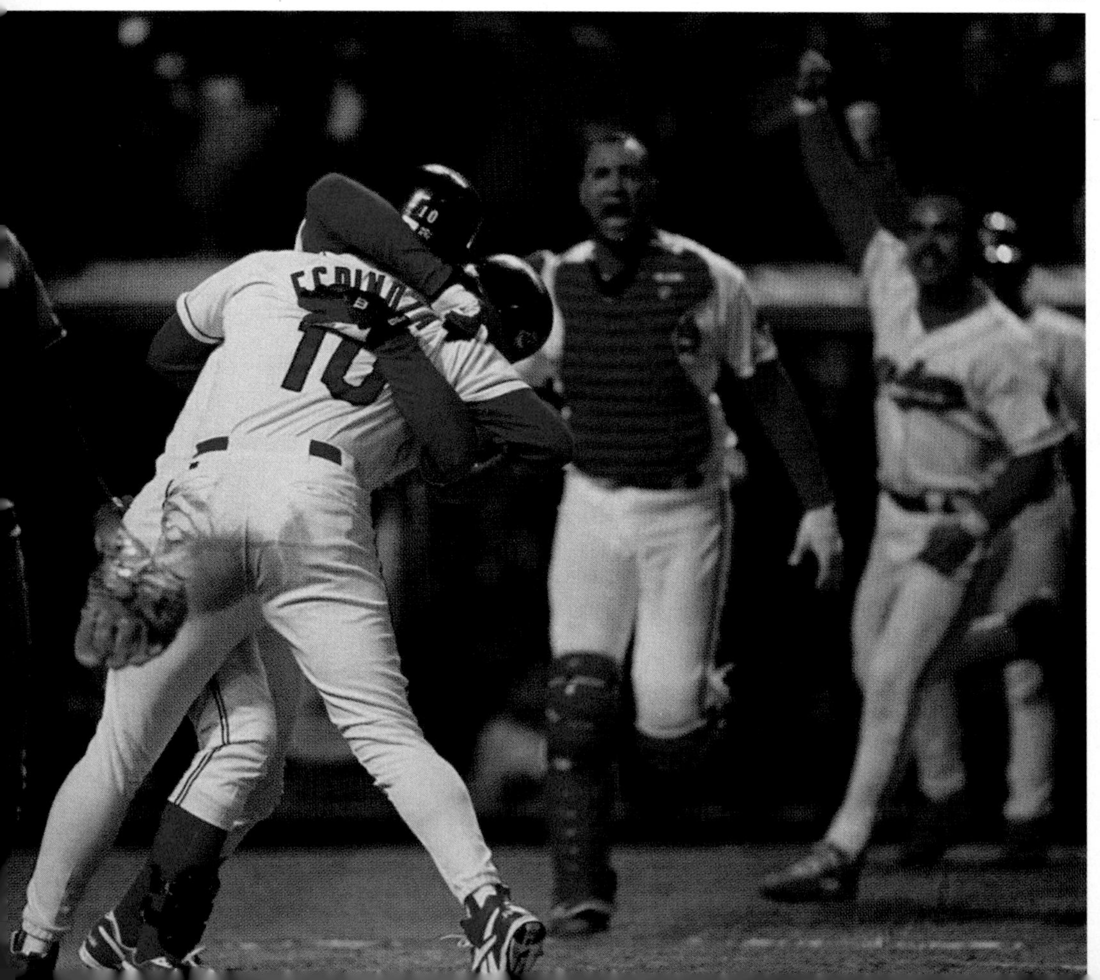

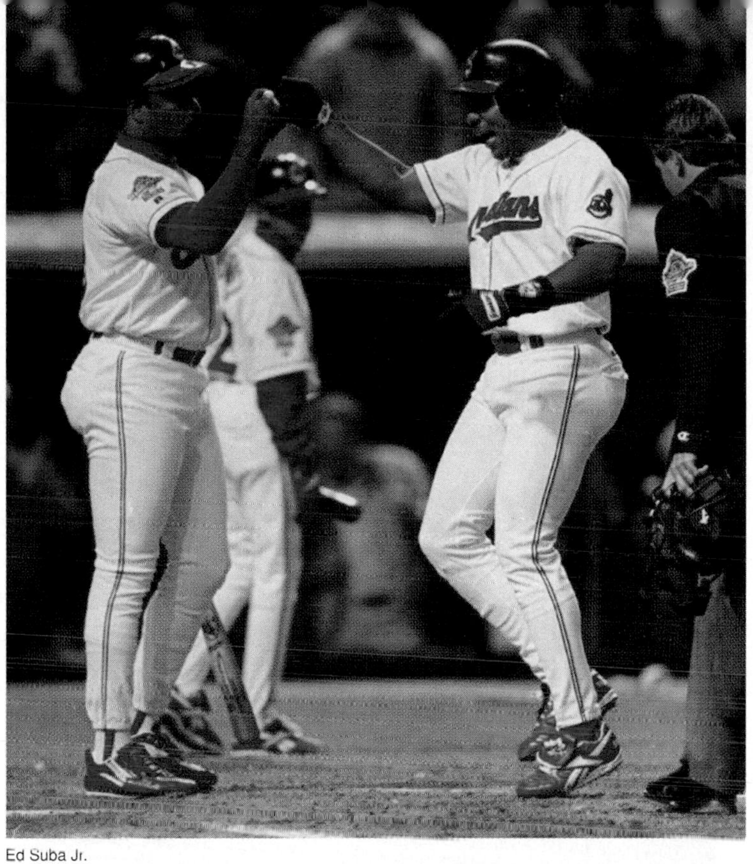

Albert Belle gives a high five to Eddie Murray after hitting a single-run homer in the sixth inning of Game 4 of the World Series. Though Belle's home run temporarily tied the game, the Indians eventually lost, 5-2.

Ed Suba Jr.

Eddie Murray has words for Atlanta Braves pitcher Greg Maddux after a fastball nearly hit Murray in the head in Game 5. Home plate umpire Frank Pulli moves to restrain him.

Phil Masturzo

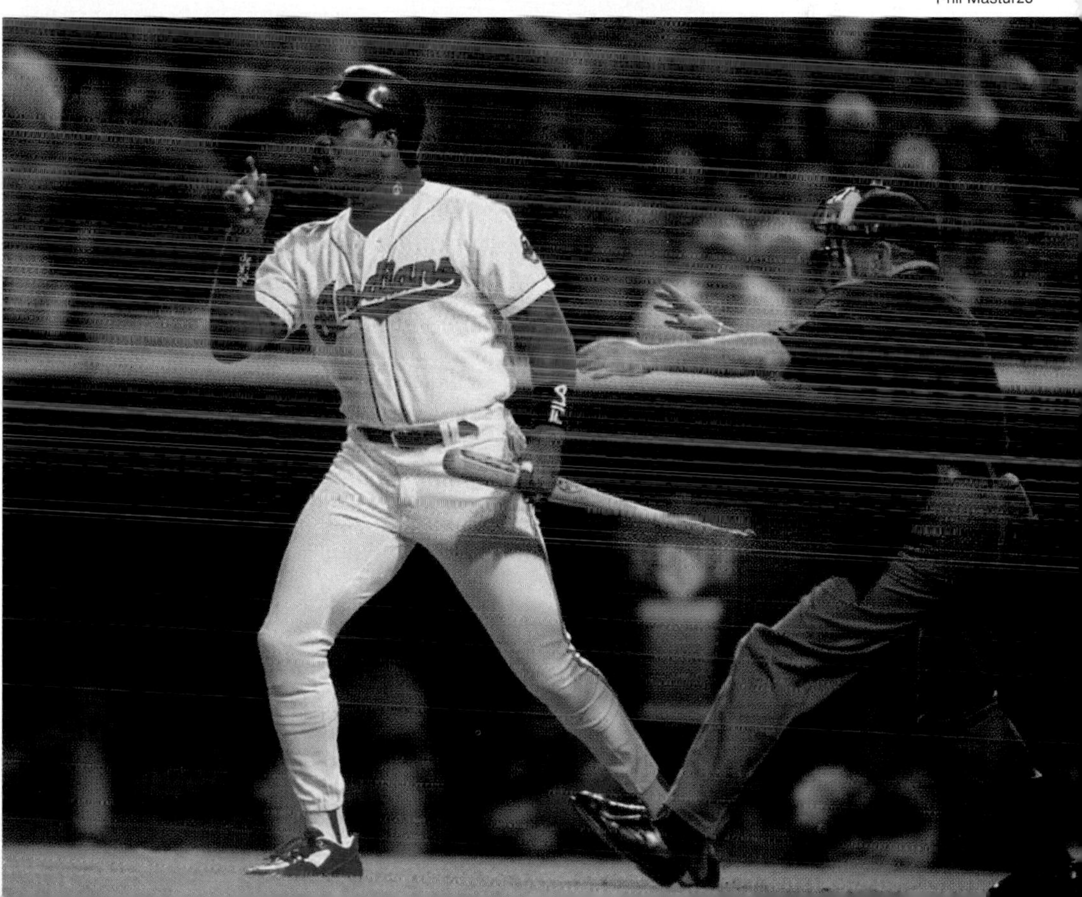

After turning a double play in Game 5, Orel Hershiser displays the kind of intensity that earned him the nickname, "The Bulldog." The World Series game was Hershiser's eighth post-season win.

Phil Masturzo

Phil Masturzo

Indians Manager Mike Hargrove consults with Jose Mesa on the mound after Mesa gave up a two-run homer in the ninth inning of Game 5. Despite the homer, the Indians beat the Braves, 5-4, for their second win of the World Series.

Ed Suba Jr.

Second baseman Carlos Baerga leaps to avoid Ryan Klesko after throwing to first to complete a double play in Game 6. Atlanta won the game, 1-0, and the World Series, four games to two.

Ed Suba Jr.

Cleveland General Manager John Hart discusses the Indians' loss in Game 6 that ended their quest for a world championship.

Lew Stamp

Eddie Murray reaches out to touch fans behind a fence at Cleveland-Hopkins International Airport. A World Series defeat didn't stop thousands of people from showing up at 3 in the morning to greet the Indians as they returned from Atlanta.

Lew Stamp

Omar Vizquel displays a boyish charm as he speaks to 40,000 fans at a post-Series Indians rally in downtown Cleveland.

behind him. It was his version of Rocky Balboa dashing through the streets of Philadelphia before the big fight with Apollo Creed.

Ramirez's high school had a very crude weight room, but Manny was a regular visitor, lifting whatever was there.

He also thought about hitting.

Watch Ramirez. Yes, there are lapses when he forgets the count. But how often does he swing at pitches that are outside the strike zone? How often is he even fooled by a pitch?

That is what astounded the scouts — his maturity at bat for one barely 18.

Joe DeLucca convinced his boss, former Tribe scouting director Mickey White, to check out Ramirez. Then White returned to Cleveland, rhapsodizing about this Dominican kid in New York, demanding that General Manager John Hart personally take a look.

Hart tells the story of walking up to an old ballfield where Manny's team played. It was during batting practice. Hart didn't even know who was hitting — he just walked into the park, a good 300 feet from the plate. But he heard a clap, the kind of sound that only comes when the bat meets the ball perfectly — spanking it in the sweet spot, as some baseball people say.

"Is that Manny?" Hart asked.

"Who else?" White replied.

It didn't take long for Hart to become a believer, too.

The Indians had the 13th pick in the 1991 draft. Think back to 1991. The Tribe was terrible, on the way to losing a franchise-record 105 games. The Indians had to have help, and the cavalry had better come to the rescue quickly. A high school kid from New York who couldn't speak English and might take years in the minors to develop — well, that wasn't exactly a quick fix.

But White insisted that the Indians draft Ramirez: He was going to be a superstar; he had quick wrists like Hank Aaron. If the Indians passed on this guy, White said, they'd regret it for the next 15 years.

The Indians considered several college players, guys who might need only a year or two in the minors before making it to Cleveland.

Sure, some of them might become good players, White said. But Ramirez, he would be a star.

Over and over, White made his case. Hart tended to agree with White. His eyes and his gut both told him that Ramirez had The Gift. Hart was then assistant to team president Hank Peters, and Peters was planning to retire at the end of the 1991 season. He had designated Hart as his successor. Peters wanted input on the 1991 amateur draft, but in the end the call would be made by Hart, White and farm director Dan O'Dowd.

A college player appeared to be the safer, wiser, and more conservative choice. That is why many of the teams drafting ahead of the Tribe passed on Ramirez.

But the Indians didn't need safe; they needed a star. White was sold on the guy. Hart and O'Dowd heard the same song. The Indians rolled the dice. They pulled the trigger. Whatever cliche you want to use, They Followed Their Hearts And Did The Right Thing.

They took Ramirez.

If nothing else, the Indians knew they would sign Manny. Back in 1989, they had selected an outfielder named Calvin Murray in the first round, and Murray had priced himself so high that the Indians couldn't fit him into their budget. Murray returned for another year of college.

Ramirez was not about to skip baseball for Yale, especially since he hadn't earned his high school diploma. Two days after drafting him, the Indians signed Manny for $300,000.

The Tribe brought him to town and set up a workout at Baldwin Wallace College so the media could see the new top draft pick. The Indians knew that English was Manny's second language — a distant second. So they hired Rod Carew to help translate and give background at the press conference. A Hall of Famer, Carew had attended Ramirez's high school (as had Henry Kissinger, by the way), and he talked about the kid, the school, the neighborhood.

For his part, a nervous Ramirez hit a few balls hard and was very shaky in the outfield drills to show off his skills. Scouting director Mickey White was there, talking about Ramirez's determination and how he "graded above-average in virtually every category."

Manny came off as exactly what he was — a terrified high school kid who had never been anywhere but New York and the Dominican Republic.

"We can talk all we want about Manny," White said. "But we just have to wait three or four years and see if we are right."

With those words, the Indians sent Ramirez to Burlington, N.C.

Ramirez had batted .650 during his senior year in high school. When he was hitting .250 during his first month as a pro, he felt like he was a hit. He ran up an $800 phone bill during that first month in North Carolina, calling home and talking forever to anyone who would listen. He was worried, frightened and lonely. One day, he went 0-for-4. In the clubhouse after the game, he announced: "I'm going home. I can't hit here."

His teammates and coaches preached patience. Manny also was pouting because he was a third baseman and a centerfielder in high school. He thought he was a great defensive player. But Manny at third? He would have needed to wear shin guards and a catcher's mask to play there without being killed. Manny in center? You've got to be kidding.

Ramirez said little to those who criticized his glove work, but his body language screamed: "What do you mean, you don't like my defense? What do you know?"

The Indians pointed Ramirez to right field and told him to go to work. Sometimes he did; often he didn't. Eventually Ramirez started to hit, and he ended up batting .326 with 19 homers in only 59 games during that 1991 season at Burlington.

Everywhere the Indians sent Manny, he hit. He opened the 1993 season at Class AA Canton-Akron. In 89 games, he had 17 homers and 79 RBI and was batting .340 in the Eastern League, a league considered deadly for most hitters. In the middle of the season, the Tribe moved him up to Class AAA Charlotte, where he batted .317 with 14 homers in 40 games.

But at Canton-Akron, he was benched a few times for failing to run out balls and for seeming asleep in the outfield. In one game a fly ball hit him in the chest and bounced about 20 feet away. Ramirez went down as if he had been shot. When he got up, he walked to the ball. By the time he picked it up, the runner had scored. It was a four-base error!

When he was promoted to Charlotte, the Tribe assigned coach Donnell Nixon to room with Ramirez, home and away. Nixon was shocked to see Manny just leave his clothes all over the place. If he dropped something, he never bothered to pick it up. At home, his sisters did that for him. He had The Gift; there was no need to trouble Manny with something as mundane as putting his socks in the dirty-clothes basket.

Ramirez had used some of his bonus money to buy a BMW, but he racked up so many traffic tickets when he played in Canton that he couldn't take the car with him to Charlotte because his license was suspended.

While Ramirez was in the process of becoming the 1993 Minor League Player of the Year, the Indians kept saying that they could wait for him. No reason to rush him to Cleveland. Let him go to spring training in 1994 and try to make the team.

Then came Sept. 1, 1993.

John Hart changed his mind. Just as he gambled when he agreed to draft Ramirez, he did so again by bringing the kid to Cleveland for a taste of the big leagues — less than three years out of George Washington High.

In his second major league game, Ramirez hammered two home runs and was 3-for-4 at Yankee Stadium. More than 60 of his friends and relatives were in the stands; Yankee Stadium is only 15 minutes by subway from his home. His friends carried banners. They blew horns. They danced in the aisles when he rounded the bases.

And, yes, he was front-page news in the New York Times again.

But after that game, Ramirez was 6-for-45.

One day, Manager Mike Hargrove wrote his name in the lineup. Manny said he couldn't play. Hargrove asked why.

"I have a sore throat," Ramirez said.

Hargrove scratched Ramirez for that night — and for the rest of the week.

The Indians asked Ramirez to work on his outfield defense. Sometimes his answer was yes; other times it was no.

"We didn't have any baby-sitters for him here," Hargrove said at the end of the 1993 season. "I honestly think that Manny can become a decent outfielder because he is a very gifted athlete, but he has to want to pay the price to do that. Right now, our plan is for him to open in Charlotte in 1994."

Ramirez hooked up with young Dominican pitcher Julian Tavarez. Neither had a clue about life in Cleveland, or the value of a dollar. One day, they asked Beacon Journal baseball writer Sheldon Ocker to lend them $60,000.

"What do you want that for?" Ocker asked.

"We want to buy motorcycles," Ramirez said.

Ocker tried to explain a couple of things: First, motorcycles don't cost $60,000. Second, sportswriters don't have $60,000, and if they did, they wouldn't carry that kind of cash around in their wallets.

Ramirez didn't get it. Hey, in American baseball everyone is a millionaire, right? So that has to go for the writers, too.

Hart wasn't concerned that Ramirez was struggling.

"Having Manny face adversity was what he needed," Hart said. "I brought him to Cleveland figuring that everything would not go smoothly. I wanted Manny to see that he didn't have it made, and then I wanted to see how he'd react to that."

Ramirez played winter ball in the Dominican Republic, where the captain of the Aguilas team was veteran catcher Tony Pena. When Pena caught Ramirez waltzing to first base or dozing in the outfield, he verbally dressed down Manny in front of his teammates. Pena is a national hero in the Dominican Republic. He also is a good person who realized that Ramirez could squander The Gift. Pena preached defense and self-discipline. Manny began to hear him. He didn't always listen, but he realized that he had to pay attention to a man such as Tony Pena.

When John Hart scouted the Dominican Republic, he saw the relationship developing between Ramirez and Pena. Hart was looking for a backup catcher, and one of the names on his list was Pena. After Hart saw the veteran and the kid in action, Pena's became the only name on the list.

The signing of Pena was one of the unnoticed, but important moves that helped build the Indians powerhouse in 1995. Not only was Pena a good influence on Ramirez, he filled in admirably for the ever-injured Sandy Alomar.

When he reported to spring training in 1994, Ramirez told Hargrove that he planned to make the team and that he'd do anything the manager wanted.

Hargrove talked defense, and for the first time he sensed that Ramirez actually was listening. He assigned Manny to coach Dave Nelson, and every day the two men practiced early. The course was Outfield Play 101: Here is the ball, here is the glove, and here is how we stand as we catch the ball.

Ramirez is blessed with tremendous hand-eye coordination. It was obvious when he was at bat, and there was no reason to believe that it wouldn't be an asset to him when he wore a glove. By the end of spring training, Ramirez had convinced Hart that he was ready, but Hargrove wasn't sure. He believed Ramirez had made major strides in the field, but worried that Manny might quit pushing himself if he made the team. Hargrove thought about it for a week. In the end, he agreed with Hart — Ramirez would play opening day for the Indians in right field.

In 1994, there still were a few scary episodes in right field. But a bigger problem was his baserunning. Often, he just seemed to keep running until someone eventually tagged him out. Other times, his mind would drift to other matters and he'd be picked off base.

But by the time the 1994 strike came, Ramirez had hit .269 with 17 homers and 60 RBI in 91 games. He was second to Kansas City's Bob Hamelin in the Rookie of the Year voting.

During the strike, Ramirez was arrested on DUI charges; he also had some other traffic violations. Hart had been trying to convince Ramirez to move to Cleveland. He considered Manny to be a good person, but one who could be led astray by his old buddies from New York. Hart was able to use the scrape with the law to show Ramirez that he needed a change of scenery.

Before the 1995 season, Manny moved into a townhouse in North Olmsted, a quiet suburb on the west side of Cleveland. To Ramirez, it seemed like Mars compared to Washington Heights. One of his sisters, a 4-year-old niece and his parents moved in with him during the summer. That made it easier for him to deal with his new home, and it saved him a lot of money when the monthly phone bills arrived.

Ramirez continued to improve in the field. Of the Indians outfielders, he may be the most consistent when it comes to throwing to the cutoff man. Often he appears to have misjudged a ball, only to lift his glove and nonchalantly spear it at the last moment.

Is he a great outfielder? Not even close. Can the Indians live with him in right field? Certainly. He continued to work with Nelson in 1995, and he should become better than average.

At the plate in 1995, The Gift kicked in. He batted .308 with 31 homers and 107 RBI. Not bad for a 23-year-old. Those home runs were no accidents. Ramirez discovered that he loves to lift weights, and he has been doing so daily. He's 6 feet tall and nearly 200 pounds of muscle.

"Look at what he's done, and he's still a baby," said Detroit Manager Sparky Anderson. "He could develop into a monster."

For Ramirez, not everything will be as simple as swinging the bat. After the strike, the Indians tried to entice him to take English lessons from Community Relations Director Allen Davis. Manny's best friend, Tavarez, reveled in the opportunity and learned to speak wonderful English. Ramirez went a few times, but displayed little interest.

Since the day they signed Ramirez, the Indians have called him a Work In Progress. He was chastised a couple of times in 1995 for base-running blunders, for forgetting the count, and for other signs of simple empty-headedness.

But, overall, the Indians have a player in Manny Ramirez who could become the greatest hitter in the history of the franchise. All they have to do is help keep him on course.

12

THE MAN WHO LOVES NUMBERS

Aug. 31, 1995: When Albert Belle doesn't hit a home run to win a game for the Indians, well, that's news. He did it on Aug. 31 — a two-run shot in the bottom of the 10th inning to give the Indians a 6-4 victory over Toronto. He also did it the night before, when his homer in the bottom of the 14th powered the Indians to a 4-3 victory over those same Blue Jays. And he did it on July 14, a grand slam homer in the bottom of the ninth. That came off Lee Smith, one of the best relievers ever. Smith had Belle down in the count: two strikes, no balls. California was winning, 5-3. But Belle crushed a hanging slider over the center field wall, more than 420 feet from the plate. Or, as Smith said, "Albert hit that ball into the barbecue pit."

With Albert Belle, you never know.

There are fans who will tell you stories of how Belle showed up unannounced at a charity event or a hospital and then spent an hour signing autographs and campaigning for Good Guy Of The Year.

Other fans tell a story like this one: "My 8-year-old son saw Albert in a store here in Euclid. He went up to him and said, 'Mr. Belle, can I have your autograph?' Belle glared at him and said, 'How much money do you have?' There was no one else around, and Albert just walked away."

Belle complains about his lack of exposure, yet forgets to wake up and attend the press conference on a new candy bar bearing his name. Rather than own up to his mistake — which caused people to wait an hour before they realized he was missing in action — Belle said that the people handling the event should have known better than to have the press conference in the morning, "because I need my rest after a night game."

Yet, Belle is one of the first Indians to arrive at the park. He spends as much time in the weight room as any of the players. He works on his hitting constantly, and believes that he doesn't receive proper respect for the effort he puts into his job. He even keeps file cards on various pitchers — what they throw him and what he does against different pitches.

But when the Plain Dealer's Bud Shaw wrote a story complimenting Belle for his diligence, dedication, and record-keeping (something few players do), Belle was enraged, screaming that Shaw had been rummaging through his locker.

Shaw denied it.

Belle demanded to know how he knew about the note cards.

"Mike Hargrove told me," Shaw said. "The batting coach told me. I didn't even look at your locker."

The coaches told Shaw about the record-keeping because they wished more players would follow Belle's lead. Instead, Belle just kept screaming obscenities (vulgar even by baseball's bawdy standards) at Shaw.

Every reporter and fan who comes in contact with Belle seems to have a story.

There have been a few times when Belle sat down with me for close to an hour, discussing hitting and baseball history. Belle is impressive because he knows that the game didn't begin on the day when he first put on a uniform. He even knows that Hank Greenberg was the last player to drive in 100 runs by the All-Star break — one of Belle's goals.

There probably aren't 10 other big leaguers today who have even heard of Hank Greenberg, the legendary Detroit slugger and later general manager of the Indians for part of the 1950s.

This is the historical reference of many players:

Once, I was interviewing Jose Mesa in Minnesota. It was the weekend that Eddie Murray was going for his 3,000th hit. Mesa was telling me a very funny story about how he gave up Robin Yount's 3,000th hit in 1993 and how he was convinced that catcher Junior Ortiz told Yount which pitch was coming.

"Hey, Jose, don't talk to him," Kenny Lofton screamed from across the room.

Mesa stopped.

"These reporters, they won't get anything right," Lofton yelled. "They never covered a guy with 3,000 hits before, and they will just screw everything up."

Mesa and I thought Lofton was kidding, but he persisted. It must be noted that Lofton was the only other person in the dressing room. It was several hours before the game. Lofton wasn't even playing that night because of a leg injury.

But he kept yelling about 3,000 hits, trying to torpedo my interview with Mesa.

Finally, Lofton said to me, "What do you know about 3,000 hits?"

"I covered Tris Speaker when he got his," I yelled to Lofton.

Lofton was puzzled. He might have heard of Speaker, the great Indians centerfielder. Then again, maybe not. He certainly had no idea that Speaker's 3,000th hit was back in 1925. He was puzzled by the whole thing, and he finally walked out of the room.

Albert Belle can tell you about Tris Speaker, or any of the game's great players. He once spent almost an hour before a game in Kansas City asking everyone about George Brett and what made Brett such a terrific hitter.

But on other days, Belle is sullen and angry, even with his own teammates. Everyone has learned just to give him plenty of room. His anger can flash suddenly, for no logical reason, at very undeserving targets. On the day he was named to the 1995 All-Star team, I didn't realize Albert was having One Of Those Days.

I approached him and said, "Albert, how about the whole outfield making the All-Star team?"

"Is that supposed to be bad?" Belle said.

"No, it sounds good to me," I said. "What do you think about it?"

"Get away from my locker," he replied.

Earlier that day, ABC's Lesley Visser wanted to interview Belle about his All-Star selection. He just got up and walked away, not saying a word.

"The least you can do is be polite," Visser said.

"What do I care about polite?" was Belle's response.

So there you are.

In Kansas City, a fan caught Belle's 46th home run. After the game, the fan brought it to the Indians clubhouse. He thought Albert might want it, and all the fan asked for in return was another autographed ball.

Belle strangely refused to sign a ball for the fan.

Stories like these force even those who know and like Belle to ask: "What's the deal with Albert?"

His blues are even a joke on the team. Last season, a reporter was asking Sandy Alomar — one of the nicest men, ever — about all his injuries. This was not one of Alomar's favorite subjects. He talked about it for a while, and the reporter persisted with more questions. Finally, Alomar said, "You know, I could be a jerk about this whole thing, like Albert."

At that point, Belle walked by Alomar's locker. He heard the line and all he did was smile.

So who is Albert Belle?

He's a man who likes to do crossword puzzles because he says it increases his vocabulary. He also likes to play chess. He isn't afraid to read, and he loves numbers. There is some depth to this man.

His mother was a high school math teacher and later a guidance counselor. His father was a high school coach and physical education teacher.

"Before we could go out and play, we had to get our homework done first," Belle said. "No excuses. You had to do it."

"We" is Albert and his brother Terry. They are fraternal twins, and Terry is a certified public accountant.

Why is Terry an accountant?

Because he heard Albert talk so excitedly about the subject that he decided to check it out, and it became his passion and profession.

At Huntington High in Shreveport, Albert had the fourth-highest grade point average in his class. In fifth place was Terry. Both took 15 credits of college work at LSU-Shreveport during their senior years in high school.

The brothers competed everywhere, even in school. Often they were in the same classes. Terry Belle told Beacon Journal columnist Jewell Cardwell that he'd wait until Albert went to bed and then check to see how far Albert had read in a book both needed for a course. If Albert had stopped on page 227 and Terry was at page 200, then Terry would stay up and read to page 228.

Albert did the same with Terry, whether the arena happened to be the classroom, the baseball diamond, or a chessboard.

"We won lots of awards from summer reading programs," Terry said. "We both loved autobiographies."

In the Belle home, there were standards and direction. You were supposed to succeed. You were to work hard, whether the subject was math or baseball.

So in high school, Belle was a star student and athlete. Hundreds of colleges wanted him, but he signed with Louisiana State in Baton Rouge. It was relatively close to home, and Coach Skip Bertman had one of the best college programs in the country.

Terry also was a baseball player, and both were recruited by LSU to play the outfield. Terry played for four years. "He was a good player for us, but not quite a pro prospect," Bertman recalled.

No problem. Terry Belle went on to earn his MBA. He's an account executive with International Paper in Memphis. But he insists, "Albert is smarter in math than I am."

When he enrolled at LSU, Belle was still known as "Joey," short for his middle name of Jojuan. To his friends from Louisiana, he is still Joey.

"He comes from a middle-class, maybe even an upper-middle-class home," Bertman said. "When I met his parents, I knew in five minutes that these people were very serious about his education, and so was Joey. It was a home with a lot of discipline and a lot of love. I never had a problem with him off the field. He took challenging courses and did well. He is a good person."

A good person with a bad temper.

"In his sophomore year with us, Joey knew that a lot of scouts were around," Bertman said. "He always put a lot of pressure on himself, but he became even more demanding of himself. You could understand why the scouts loved him — he was big, strong, fast, athletic and motivated."

During his sophomore year, Belle batted .354. But more eye-popping were his 21 homers and 66 RBI in 243 at bats. Heading into his junior year, he was projected as a No. 1 draft pick.

"He had days where he wouldn't run out a pop-up, or he'd throw equipment after a strikeout," Bertman said. "He never loafed when it came to running down a ball in the outfield or breaking up a double play. He is a tremendous competitor."

But Bertman felt compelled to suspend Belle during his junior year.

Earlier in the season, Bertman believed Belle had protested a called third strike for far too long. In another game, he had failed to run out a fly ball.

"After the second incident, I told Joey that if something happened again, he was finished for the rest of the season," Bertman said. "I didn't want to do it, but I wasn't going to make exceptions for him."

LSU was facing Mississippi State in the Southeastern Conference tournament. Like many episodes in Belle's life, there are different versions of what happened.

The first is that an obnoxious fan was yelling racial taunts at Belle, and Belle took off after the fan. (This has been repeated so often that it is taken as fact in many places.) For his behavior, Belle was suspended for the remainder of the season and the College World Series.

But Bertman said that wasn't what happened.

According to the coach, a fan was standing in right field — in an area that was restricted, not open to any fans. Belle told an usher, who relayed the news to a policeman. The man was taken out of the area, and he screamed at Belle.

"Now, people say that was a racial incident, but it wasn't," Bertman said. "Nor was that why I suspended him."

What was the reason?

"In the same game, he hit a ball that he thought was out of the park, and he went into his home-run trot," Bertman said. "The ball hit against the wall and all he got out of it was a single. I had to suspend him at that point, because I had said there would be no more incidents like that where he didn't run hard. I had talked to him several times about this subject. I had community leaders and counselors talk to him, and all of them came away saying what a fine young man he was. We had tried discipline, hugs and patience. I didn't know what else to do. I know his family was really upset with me, because they thought I hurt his standing in the draft. But I felt that I had no choice."

So the red flag was raised next to Belle's name in the draft rooms of many teams. Atlanta Manager Bobby Cox reportedly told his farm director that he'd be fired if he drafted Belle.

The year was 1987, and Belle was entering the draft after his junior year. The Indians had lost their first-round pick in another trade, and they were on course to losing 101 games. Tribe scouting director Jeff Scott brought General Manager Joe Klein to Baton Rouge, so he could personally check out Belle.

As a physical specimen, Klein had no doubts: "He was among the top three picks in the entire draft."

They dug into his background and talked to Bertman. The coach explained his reason for the suspension. He said that Belle had no problems with drinking, drugs or other off-the-field troubles. They learned of his solid home, his excellent school work and his strong family values.

"The majors are full of guys who have had problems like Albert," Klein told Scott. "If he's there, let's take him."

He was, and the Indians signed him for $65,000. While John Hart's administration deserves the lion's share of the credit for the Tribe's revival, it also must be remembered that a gutsy move by two guys who did their homework — Klein and Scott — delivered a player to the Tribe who may end up as the best power hitter in the history of the franchise.

Belle's rise to Cleveland was like a volcano, full of sparks, smoke and heat.

Mike Hargrove was his first manager at Class A Kinston, N.C., and in the Florida instructional league in the winter of 1987-88. Hargrove recalled Belle as "showing no personality, being very withdrawn."

There was an afternoon game in Florida when Belle hit a line drive to the shortstop. "You couldn't hit a ball any harder," Hargrove said. "But it went right to the shortstop. The guy barely had to move his glove."

Belle ran to first base and kept running. He ran all the way out of the park and into a nearby orange grove, and this happened right in the middle of a game! Hargrove remembers that Belle didn't return until after 7 p.m., still in his uniform several hours after the game was over.

"He had been beating himself up mentally the whole time," Hargrove said.

Belle came to Cleveland fast — too fast.

He was promoted in the middle of the 1989 season, direct from Class AA Canton-Akron. He skipped Class AAA. He had played only 149 pro games over three years — a single season's worth in terms of experience. Belle was hitting a respectable .282 at Canton, and the Indians were enamored of his 20 homers in 89 games.

So to Cleveland he went, where he played for a terrible team in a lineup where he was exposed as one of the few power threats. He batted only .225 with seven homers in 62 games.

Hindsight is always clear, and several members of the Indians front office said Belle wasn't ready and hadn't earned such a quick promotion. They mentioned his immaturity on the field, the sulking and temper tantrums. He also was embarrassing in left field. But even more critical, he had a major flaw at bat. Most hitters step *into* the pitch, but Belle stepped *away*. He did that because he was trying to pull everything over the left-field wall. In Class AA, pitchers had made mistakes; their control wasn't sharp, and when they threw the ball inside, Belle hit it so hard that he made it beg for mercy. But he was almost helpless when confronted with breaking pitches on the outside corner, and he was being platooned by the end of the 1989 season.

Belle opened the 1990 season with Cleveland, but hit only .174. After nine games he was shipped to Class AAA Colorado Springs, which is where he should have played in the second half of 1989 instead of Cleveland.

But now, Albert was angry. He thought the Indians had given up on him too soon, and he may have had a point because he batted only 23 times before being demoted. Bob Molinaro had managed Belle at Canton in 1989, and he had him again in Colorado Springs in 1990. He was used to Belle's moods and outbursts, but he was growing more worried about Albert's self-destructive behavior.

Some games, he didn't run out balls. Other times, he was totally disinterested in the outfield. He was hitting .328, but he became enraged after making outs, throwing bats and helmets.

One day, Belle made an out and returned to the dugout. He took his bat and began pounding the dugout sink so viciously that it was frightening. Then he went to the outfield, and during a game of catch between innings, he heaved a ball over the fence.

Things were so out of control that even Albert Belle knew something had to give.

In the summer of 1990, Belle entered Cleveland Clinic's alcohol and drug rehabilitation program. Drugs were never an issue, but Belle said he had a drinking problem.

Once again, there's more than one version of the story.

His college coach, Skip Bertman, said he never noticed Belle drinking.

LSU teammate and veteran big-league pitcher Ben McDonald said he once saw Belle strike out and heave his bat halfway up the screen against home plate. He also saw Belle smash a helmet against a wall. But he never saw Belle drunk.

His minor league manager, Bob Molinaro, has a book's worth of stories about Belle's temper, but remembers him playing chess and reading the Bible, not hanging out in bars or looking hung over the next day.

His closest friend in the Tribe farm system, coach Billy Williams, also was surprised when Belle announced he was an alcoholic.

Hank Peters was the Indians president in 1990, and he didn't see signs of a drinking problem. But if Belle wanted help, the Indians were thrilled to lend him a hand.

His family was shocked. They remembered Albert as an Eagle Scout, a good student and son.

Belle said he was a closet drinker. He said that he poured down a gut-buster known as Gorilla's Breath, equal parts of 151-proof rum and 101-proof Wild Turkey. He told friends that he had "another life" and booze was a big part of it.

Certainly Belle took his rehabilitation seriously. He left after the first few days because he found himself in a room with a bunch of middle-aged cocaine and heroin addicts, and he didn't see how that related to him and his demons. But he returned to the Cleveland Clinic the next day, determined to face his troubles.

It usually is a 30-day program, but Belle stayed in for three months until he was sure that he had a handle on his life. He met former Indian Andre Thornton, who was doing counseling and ministry at the Clinic. The two men became friends, and his relationship with Thornton remains a key to his success.

Belle went into Cleveland Clinic as Joey, and came out calling himself Albert — his given first name. To him, it was a symbol of his new life.

Everything has not been smooth for Belle, but every year also seems a little better than the last.

In 1991, he batted .282 with 28 homers for the Tribe. He also was sent to the minors for a month for several episodes of not hustling.

In 1992, he hit .260 with 34 homers and 112 RBI. In 1993, he raised the average to .290 with 38 homers and 129 RBI, but he also was suspended for throwing a baseball at the chest of an unruly fan.

Early in his Cleveland career, Mike Hargrove would call Belle in to either chastise or discuss his transgressions on the field — usually not hustling. Belle would sit there like a 6-foot-2, 220-pound stone, not saying a word. The next day, the manager would arrive in his office and find a check that Belle had written to pay the fine levied the night before. Again, nothing was said.

The Indians hope Belle will continue to work out ways to express himself — ways other than raw anger. But of Belle at the plate, they have no complaints.

"Everyone in baseball knew that Albert would hit a lot of home runs," said Frank Robinson, the Hall of Famer and Orioles general manager. "But I don't think many saw him as a .300 hitter. That is what has really impressed me about Albert — how he has matured at the plate. Now he doesn't chase those outside pitches. He'll take them, or he hits them to right field. He is very disciplined up there."

Belle constantly worked on his hitting, especially his weakness of "pulling out" and stepping away when he swung the bat. When he hit .357 with 36 homers and 101 RBI in the strike-marred 1994 season, it was clear Belle could do everything at the plate. He hit for power, he hit for average, and each year his strikeouts were going down as his walk totals rose.

He also improved in left field, although he still had an annoying habit of missing the cutoff man with throws.

Until the 1995 season, Belle seemed to be suspended every year for throwing a ball at a fan or charging a pitcher he thought was throwing at him.

In 1994, there was Batgate in Chicago. The White Sox asked the umpires to inspect Belle's bat. They took it, and the next day some dimwit with the Indians stole the bat from the umpires' room, replacing it with a Paul Sorrento model.

This meant one of two things: The dimwit who did the bat switch couldn't read, or all of Belle's bats were filled illegally with cork and the Indians had to find someone's bat that was legal.

Anyway, the switch fooled no one. A Belle bat was turned over to the umpires. The American League cut it open and discovered it was corked. Belle was suspended for seven games, but he maintains his innocence to this day, insisting that the White Sox stole his bats in the dead of night, corked them and put them back in the Tribe's dressing room. Maybe Oliver Stone would buy it, but it seems a stretch.

After the 1994 season, Life magazine reported that a Belle bat was a prize at a charity auction. The fan who won the bat had it x-rayed — and it was corked. There were even rumors that Belle had used a corked bat in the Cape Cod League, a summer showcase for the top college players.

Corked or not, Belle can hit. As Skip Bertman said, "He can hit home runs with a matchstick." After Batgate, Belle batted .476 (30-for-63) with 10 homers in 20 games before the strike ended the 1994 season.

It was in 1994 that Belle became one of the game's most feared clutch hitters, hammering four game-winning homers in his last at-bat. That is a staggering statistic. In 1995, it was more of the same.

As was mentioned before, Belle loves numbers. He knows that he's the first Indian to hit at least 30 homers in four consecutive seasons. He even knows that he batted .479 when he hit the first pitch during the 1994 season. He had his eye on the Indians record of 43 homers by Al Rosen in 1953 and broke it with 50 in 1995. His next goal is the career mark of 226 homers by Earl Averill. Belle already has 194 homers, and he won't turn

30 until August of 1996. In 1995, he became the first player in baseball history to hit 50 homers and 50 doubles in the same season, and he led the American League in home runs (50), runs scored (121), slugging percentage (.690), total bases (377), extra-base hits (103), doubles (52) and RBI (126).

Belle has his idiosyncrasies:

1. When No. 3 hitter Carlos Baerga comes on deck, so does Belle.

2. He doesn't leave the on-deck circle until his name is announced.

3. Every Tribe hitter has a personal theme song when he comes to bat, but Belle demands silence after his name.

4. He erases the back line of the batter's box, as if he's saying the box can't hold him.

5. After every pitch, Belle steps out of the box and takes two swings — never one, never three, just two.

6. When Belle hits a home run, he does the Albert Shuffle. He jogs to first base and steps on the bag — nothing special. About 10 feet from second base, he does a quick shake-and-bake dance with his feet, then steps on the bag. He repeats that before hitting third base and home plate.

Belle is obsessive about his bats.

His favorite model is a Louisville Slugger, No. B343. It is 35 inches long and weighs 33 ounces. If he finds a bat he likes, he uses it until it breaks. Other players will switch bats if they are in a slump or if a bat "stops feeling right." But once Belle picks a bat, he stays with it.

If Belle receives a new bat and there is the slightest scuff or nick — forget it, he won't even try that bat. It has to be clean and new, and yet he'll keep the bat until it looks like something the dog has gnawed on.

Belle has his Number 8 written in black magic marker on the knob of each of his bats.

"Albert has his eccentricities," Hargrove said. "But I never worry about him not being mentally ready to play. It gives me a secure feeling to write his name in the fourth spot of the lineup every day."

Belle deserves enormous credit for his improvement as a hitter and for wrestling with his temper. He still has his moods when he can be downright ornery. Many teams would not have had the patience to stay with a young Albert Belle, but farm director Dan O'Dowd and General Manager John Hart believed in Belle, even though he kept them up late into the evening trying to figure out what they could do to help him. Mike Hargrove has become the first manager whom Belle seems to trust and with whom Belle has been able to establish some sort of line of communication.

Belle uses his critics to stoke his sizzling fires of desire. He talks about how some baseball people and writers insisted he didn't have the temperament to play in the majors — much less be a star — and how he loves to make them eat their words every day. He is a tough guy who doesn't let minor injuries exile him to the bench.

He also is one of the few Tribe players who lives in town all year.

Most Cleveland fans have supported Belle from his earliest and darkest days. Maybe it is because they saw his explosions as signs that at least he cared enough to get that angry, which was more than most of the players in the early 1990s were willing to do. They saw the fierce look at home plate, the sweat on his brow and his flair for the dramatic and they knew that Belle was working when he was at bat. He was fighting the pitcher, not giving in.

In the end, maybe that is the best thing that can be said about Albert Jojuan Belle — he never gave in.

13

An Eagle On The Mound

Sept. 8, 1995: At 11:02 p.m., the Indians clinched the Central Division title — their first title of any type in 41 years. They beat Baltimore, 3-2. Orel Hershiser was the winning pitcher. Eddie Murray had three hits and drove in two runs. Jose Mesa picked up his 40th save. The Indians' record was 86-37 and they led the division by 23½ games.

Orel Hershiser looks like a nerd, especially when he wears his glasses.

I'm not the one saying that — he is.

The Indians pitcher doesn't have muscles; he has noodles. When he takes off his shirt and looks at his chest, he says, "It's kind of concaved."

Even his name, Orel Hershiser, is . . . well, not exactly macho. It's not even a baseball name like Bucky, Lefty, Dizzy or Daffy.

He had a minor league roommate named Wickensheimer.

"We once pitched in a doubleheader and won," he said. "Wickensheimer and Hershiser. A doubleheader won by a law firm."

Kids used to tease him mercilessly about his name, and Orel himself wasn't really thrilled with it. But that changed when he was with the Dodgers and made a commercial with tennis star Martina Navratilova. She told him that Orel meant "eagle" in Czech.

He liked that. He liked that a lot. He told his father, Orel III. He later named his son Orel V. The Eagle. Now there was a name with power, a name that soared.

Those who meet Hershiser for the first time realize that he is a nice, thoughtful guy. He likes golf and the country-club set. He dresses a little preppy and knows which fork to use at a formal dinner.

That's because Hershiser comes from money. His father built a successful printing business and retired by the time he was 50. In the process, Orel III moved his family from Detroit to Buffalo to Toronto and finally to New Jersey.

Hershiser's ancestors were Hessians, and the Original Orel supposedly came to this country during the Revolutionary War. Original Orel was a hired gun — paid to fight on the side of the British. His side lost the war, but his family found a new home in the new United States.

Orel Hershiser IV sees himself as a hired gun, too. That's what he called himself after signing with the Indians as a free agent on April 8, 1995.

"I know that Cleveland has not been in a World Series for over 40 years," he said one spring afternoon in Winter Haven, Fla. "The Cleveland team that gets to the World Series is one that will be remembered forever in the city of Cleveland. I want to be a part of that team."

Hershiser was 36 when Indians General Manager John Hart signed the right-handed pitcher. He had spent 12 years with the Los Angeles Dodgers. He had won 134 games and a Cy Young Award and was the Most Valuable Player of the 1988 National League playoffs and 1988 World Series.

He was the kind of player who never would have come to Cleveland in the past, yet in the spring of 1995 he jumped at a chance to pitch for the Tribe. He brought with him a post-season record of 5-0 and a 1.47 earned-run average.

Hershiser has been Mr. October since his days with the Dodgers in the mid-1980s. But those who remember "Young O," as he was called by his family, still find this pretty hard to believe.

They'll tell you about a Hershiser who was a decent high school athlete in Cherry Hill, N.J., and who got offered a scholarship from only one major college — Bowling Green State University in Ohio.

They'll tell you how Hershiser didn't even make the Bowling Green traveling squad during his freshman season and how he became so discouraged that he stopped going to class and nearly flunked out as a sophomore.

They'll tell you that Hershiser then kicked himself in the butt, made the dean's list as a junior, and pitched well enough to be drafted by the Dodgers in the 17th round in 1979. But Hershiser will add, "I was more a suspect than a prospect."

They'll also tell you that Hershiser was 6-foot-3 and 185 pounds of skin and seemingly brittle bones. He was a relief pitcher because he didn't seem to have the right stuff to throw nine innings. In five minor league seasons, he started only 21 games.

Hershiser has a newspaper clipping from the San Antonio Light that reads: "Orel Hershiser made everyone at the ballpark hold their collective breath last season when he entered the game as a relief pitcher . . Fans never knew if he would serve the pitch that would be hit for the game-winner or the one that would retire the side."

When Hershiser finally did make the Dodgers in 1984, he had a 35-29 minor league record and an ERA slightly under 4.00. No one thought he'd stay very long.

But Orel Leonard Hershiser IV has been surprising people for a long time.

The only reason this minor league relief pitcher received a start from the Dodgers is because two other guys were hurt. One day he walked into the clubhouse at Shea Stadium in New York. Dodgers Manager Tommy Lasorda was signing a box of baseballs. Lasorda signed a ball, flipped it to Hershiser, and said, "Kid, tonight it's your ball."

Hershiser took that baseball and never let go. He discovered the sinker that Indians Manager Mike Hargrove says "is downright unhittable."

His career with the Dodgers is now Los Angeles lore. He was 19-3 with a 2.03 ERA in 1985. In 1988, he won the Cy Young Award with a 23-8 record; his 59 consecutive scoreless innings set a major league record.

He has a sense of baseball history. Those 59 scoreless innings broke a record set by another former Dodger, Don Drysdale, who pitched 58 of them in 1968. When Hershiser wiped Drysdale out of the record book, he insisted that Drysdale be in the dressing room so both men could pose for pictures and meet the press together.

It was a rare tribute — the type seldom seen from most players, who believe that the game began when they first joined the team. But Hershiser is different. He has read baseball books and he collected baseball cards all the way through high school. He is polite and gracious with fans and reporters. You spend some time with Hershiser, and you think, "If I ever become a star, I hope that I'll act like Orel."

A month into the 1990 season, Hershiser blew out his shoulder. In medical terms, he had an operation that "reconstructed the anterior capsule and tightened the ligaments." What that means is that a doctor put his shoulder back together.

"I went 13 months without pitching, and when I came back, my fastball just wasn't even close to the same," Hershiser said. "But it was more than that. When I lost my velocity, I lost some break on my curveball and my sinker just wasn't as hard."

He went from being able to throw in the low-90 mph range to the low 80-mph range. That's the difference between an above-average and a below-average fastball. And that's what separates a Cy Young Award winner from a guy who loses as often as he wins.

"My top fastball was 93 mph, but I only used it maybe five to 10 times a game," he said. "It was there when I needed to reach back for it. After the surgery, I'd reach back and it would be an 85-mph fastball. And I was throwing in the low 80s much of the time."

After the surgery, Hershiser was still a decent pitcher, but he never dominated again. Before the operation, his record with the Dodgers was 98-66; after the surgery, it was 36-36.

"When we signed Orel, we hoped he'd win 10 to 12 games for us," Hart said. "We thought he could do a little better than Jack Morris did for us in 1994 (with 10 wins). We never expected this."

What Hart didn't expect was Hershiser to be a guy who had a 16-6 record for the 1995 season, a guy who was 11-2 after the All-Star break.

Something had happened to Hershiser. At the age of 36, he was throwing like he was 26. He would uncork a fastball in the 91-mph range and then step back from the mound and think, "It's coming back; it really is."

He surprised himself with his fastball.

"Hitters keep coming up to me and saying, 'You've got the bite in your curveball . . . you've got that heavy sinker again.' That has really helped my confidence," he said. "I know that I'm throwing better, but it is great to hear it from guys on the other team."

Hershiser's 16 victories were the most for him since he was 23-8 for the Dodgers in 1988, the same season that he set a record with the 59 consecutive scoreless innings.

"Now, I can see how that happened," Hargrove said. "He has thrown some sinkers that have just disappeared. I mean, you see it — then it's gone. That is the closest thing to an unhittable pitch as I've ever seen."

Signing Orel Hershiser as a free agent for $1.4 million was one of the shrewdest moves ever made by John Hart.

"Orel's record was only 6-6 in 1994, but he left 10 games (with the Dodgers) in which he had the lead or the score was tied and he didn't get a win," Hart said. "I told him that he should come to the American League, where we wouldn't have to pinch-hit for him. We brought Orel and his wife to town. We showed them the new ballpark and took them to eat at Johnny's Restaurant (in downtown Cleveland). I told Orel, 'Start thinking about winning 15 to 16 games again; you can do that with our lineup.' "

The sales job worked, although Hershiser didn't fully comprehend the thunder of the Tribe's bats until midseason.

"That is when I had a six-game span in which I was backed by something like 66 runs," he said. "Man, you get that kind of support and you feel indestructible. Even if you are losing, you think, 'Just keep cool and keep the score close; we'll wake up and get back into this thing.' Cleveland was my Number 1 choice when I went to look for a team, and coming here has been a great move for my career."

Hershiser became the Indians' money pitcher. He beat Baltimore 3-2 on Sept. 8 to clinch the Tribe's first pennant in 41 years, and in doing so delivered on his own dream of being part of a team that will always be special in the hearts of fans.

"Put a black cape and hood on him, stick a scythe in his hand, and he looks just like the Grim Reaper," Hargrove said. "The more pressure, the more concentration he brings to the situation. Look it up: He has a history of pitching well in big games."

In 1995, Hershiser won four games in the post-season, making his lifetime record 8-1 in playoff and World Series games. And eight victories is the most any pitcher has won in the post-season.

Hargrove marveled at the right-hander, who had turned 37 by the end of the season.

"Orel staring at the plate — it was like he was a laser beam," Hargrove said. "You could just *feel* him bearing down. He is the most focused person I've ever met."

Then Hargrove told another story:

"Early in the season, I heard Orel say that in a game that wasn't close, he'd pretend it was the ninth inning of the seventh game of the World Series to help him concentrate. I thought to myself, 'Right — I bet you do.' I had real doubts. I figured that he was just talking, like some guys do. But after watching him this season, I can imagine him doing that."

And Hargrove really learned what Hershiser was talking about, as Hershiser became an even better pitcher in the post-season.

"I'm throwing harder now than at any time since my shoulder

surgery," Hershiser said. "I've gained 3 to 4 mph on my fastball since 1993. It is like all the rehabilitation and work I put into my shoulder has suddenly come back to me."

To Indians fans, this is an incredible story. It used to be that when the Indians signed someone such as Hershiser, his name was Wayne Garland and his arm nearly fell off — it didn't heal and come back better than ever.

This was yet another sign that 1995 was an Indians summer. This team not only was very good; it was lucky.

Hershiser often thinks about where he has been, about how he was the forgotten pitcher at Bowling Green and the last man on the Dodgers staff in 1984. A sincere Christian, he will read some of his favorite psalms before he pitches and he'll sing one of his favorite Christian tunes, most likely *Praise God from Whom All Blessings Flow*. Heck, he once sang this hymn on the Johnny Carson show. When he ponders his career, he drops down on his knees to give thanks for all his blessings.

Tribe fans should feel the same way.

14

TAKING CHANCES

Sept. 9, 1995: The Indians didn't need to win — after all, they had clinched the Central Division championship the night before. But the Tribe racked up another victory, beating Baltimore 2-1. Chad Ogea was the winning pitcher, Jim Thome and Alvaro Espinoza drove in the winning runs, and Jose Mesa recorded his 41st save of the season.

The morning after the Indians clinched their first title in 41 years, General Manager John Hart found himself alone at Jacobs Field.

"It was exactly how I wanted it," Hart said. "No one was there. I could walk around the park, look at the empty diamond and just think about things. That was really when it hit me, there in the quiet with the sun coming up."

Hart thought about the Indians and how he took a team that lost 105 games in 1991 and turned it into the 1995 Central Division champion. He thought about the town coming alive, about the trades that worked, and about the feeling of success.

Then Hart thought about where he had started.

"I had a cup of coffee in Class AAA, but I was basically a Class AA catcher," he said. "I was the kind of player they say is a 'good guy on the club.' I was a pretty good catcher, but I couldn't hit — .240 was it for me."

Then Hart shook his head and laughed.

"You know, I like guys with power arms and power bats — that is how the Indians are put together," he said. "Well, I never would have signed a ballplayer like me."

Instead of champagne and jet planes, Hart found himself mostly thinking about bus rides on that morning after the clinch.

"My first year as a minor league manager was in 1982 at Bluefield (W.Va.)," he said. "That was a (Class A Orioles farm) team in the

Appalachian League, as low as you can go in the minors. I had kids straight out of high school and junior college. We'd lose a tough game, and I'd stop the bus at 2 in the morning in the middle of nowhere.

"Everyone would be bleary-eyed. They probably thought I was a maniac, walking up and down the aisles of that bus, talking about the game and executing fundamentals. I'd have the team up the next morning at 9 for a special workout before the regular game. I was being paid $4,000, and I didn't even have a contract. It was just a handshake deal for that season, and that season only.

"OK, it was only rookie ball, but, buddy, I had to win. I didn't play in the big leagues. No one knew my name, and I had no one pushing me up the ladder because he was a friend of mine. It was produce or be gone."

In Bluefield, Hart banned his young team from having beer in their rooms. During bed checks, he also made sure that his players were keeping sober.

One night, he caught Billy Ripken with a can of beer. Ripken was only 18 and terrified when Hart said that was a $25 fine and they would talk more about it in the morning.

A few minutes after Hart left Ripken's room, he heard a knock on his own door. It was Ripken. The young infielder peeled off $22 with shaky hands — all in dollar bills. He had the remaining three bucks in change.

Billy's brother, Cal Jr., was a rookie with the Orioles. His father, Cal Sr., was Baltimore's third-base coach.

"You aren't going to tell my father, are you?" Ripken asked.

"Billy, you are now a professional," Hart replied. "You are going to stand up or fall down on your own. Your father has nothing to do with this."

Hart's team won the title, and he was named the 1982 Appalachian League Manager of the Year.

"Our record was 47-15, and I thought I was hot stuff," Hart said. "I said, 'Look out, Earl (Weaver), here I come to Baltimore.' "

Hart managed at every level in the Orioles farm system, and each of his teams had a winning record and made the playoffs.

In 1986, he was the Minor League Manager of the Year at Class AAA Rochester. Once again, Billy Ripken was playing for him.

"We were staying at a Budgetel in Toledo, and the motel manager woke me up at 2 in the morning to say some of my players were having a party and they wouldn't shut up," Hart said. "I went to the room and found Billy and his roommate. I told those guys to meet me in the lobby at 6 a.m."

Ripken and his friend showed up looking as if they had slept outside and not slept well. Hart said, "OK, boys, let's run." He led them on a two-mile run to a health club, where he made them lift weights.

"They sweated out everything they ever drank," Hart said.

It's the fall of 1995. Hart is 47 years old. It has been nine years since he left the driving to Greyhound and chased his major league dreams. He has a guaranteed contract through the year 2000, and Tribe owner Dick Jacobs has a two-year option on Hart when that deal is through. He was the Major League Executive of the Year in 1994, and worked his magic again by signing 16-game winner Orel Hershiser, who also was a star in the post-season.

But Hart is still that guy on the bus from Bluefield, wanting to prove himself to those who don't know him and to those who doubt that he has the right stuff.

Perhaps that is why he is so relentless.

"I hired John because he is all baseball," Jacobs said. "He eats it and sleeps it."

Actually, Hart doesn't sleep much, no more than four hours most nights. Next to his bed, he has a note pad. He'll wake in the middle of the night, turn on the light and start writing down ideas. Sandi, his wife of 24 years, has learned to ask him if he plans to stay up for a while. If he says he's in the middle of a brainstorm, she takes cover in a bed in another room.

Then, most mornings, Hart is up by 7, preparing for a 45-minute workout.

"His energy," Jacobs said. "That was why (former Tribe president) Hank Peters hired John, and it is why I moved him up after Hank retired (on Sept. 18, 1991)."

Hart had run the Indians with Peters' blessing in 1991. The team lost a franchise-record 105 games as Hart frantically shuffled bodies in and out of town. He went through 53 players — another franchise record — including 23 rookies.

"Back then, I don't think a lot of people thought I was very smart," Hart said. "They saw me and said that I was quick on the trigger, that my team had no stability. That is why I am very careful not to make too much of this year, because I know that I'm still the same person who was the dumbest guy coming down the pike only a few years ago."

When a potential trade comes up, Hart will drive nearly every member of his inner circle to the point where they want to stuff a scouting report down his throat.

"I admit it — I worry everyone to death when it comes to trades," he said. "I love the little deals, where it is announced and everyone says, 'Ho-hum.' Then it turns out to be a trade that brings you a Jose Mesa (for Kyle Washington) or a Paul Sorrento (for Curt Leskanic and Oscar Munoz)."

Guess where this restless Hart was a week before the end of the 1995 regular season. He was in Winter Haven, Fla., with the Tribe's instructional league team. He wanted to see the best prospects in the farm system.

"My fear is that we'll trade away one of these kids before we know who he is as a player," Hart said. "I wish I had spent more time in the farm system this year. I don't want us to slip. I still have memories of being up in the old Stadium office until 2 in the morning with (assistant general manager) Dan O'Dowd as we just had our asses kicked, trying to figure out how we were going to make this thing work."

Hart has no baseball pedigree; he says his father was his mentor.

John Hart Sr. was born in southern Georgia, "the kind of place with chickens running around in the yard and the screen door always slamming," Hart said. "His people came over with Oglethorpe on the old prison boats (from England)."

The seventh of seven children from a dirt-poor family, John Hart Sr. moved to the Orlando area to find something more than life on a farm. He went to work in a grocery warehouse as a laborer and ended up as president of the Associated Grocers of Florida.

"He only had a high school education, but he went toe to toe with guys with Harvard MBAs," Hart said. "He negotiated contracts with Jimmy Hoffa. My parents eloped at 18 and had me about a year later. My father never got a break because he knew someone. He just worked his way up."

The Hart family lived in Winter Park, and everything was "super" until he was 10 — that was when his parents got a divorce.

"It was a shock, and it changed my life," Hart said.

His mother remarried, this time to an Air Force colonel. Hart lived with them for a while, moving from Florida to Germany to Turkey to Alabama. During his junior year in high school, he lived with his grandmother. He also stayed close to his father. "He always has been and still is my best friend," Hart said.

As he moved from family to family — and country to country — Hart learned how to survive in different environments. That may be why he can operate as a hard-boiled, tobacco-chewing baseball man with his minor league coaches. Then he can put on a pair of yuppie suspenders and a three-piece suit and talk up-sides, down-sides and projections with the business associates of Dick Jacobs. And he can do it all in the same day.

His father had the same ability — talking the language of tattooed men who loaded trucks in the morning and then having a power lunch with the bottom-line grocery executives at noon.

Hart felt it was critical that he didn't stay in pro baseball after he was cut by the Expos in 1972. He spent the next 10 years as a high school coach, running his own baseball school and owning the first health club to have a Nautilus weight program in the Orlando area.

"You know where I did the best coaching job of my life?" he asked. "It was with a ninth grade football team. The school hadn't won a game in two years, and we went undefeated. I had high school baseball teams that won state titles, but nothing gave me as much satisfaction as that football season because I didn't know much about football."

All Hart's success in business and high school coaching did was fire the thirst for more. When the Orioles offered him a chance to manage in Bluefield in 1982, he was 33 years old. He knew it was then or never.

The same could be said when Hart took over for Hank Peters. If Hart failed with the Indians, the odds were against him ever running another big-league team.

Peters was the Orioles general manager when Hart was promoted through the farm system. Hart saw himself as another Earl Weaver — a team manager — but Peters envisioned Hart as another Hank Peters.

Peters talks about Hart's charisma, his work ethic, his creativity, and his business sense. When he hired Hart in 1989 as his assistant in Cleveland, Peters did it mostly because he had a gut feeling that there was something special about this young man who had been the Orioles third-base coach.

Because he was 63 when he was hired as Tribe president in 1987, Peters took on two jobs — building the Indians farm system and grooming a successor. He did both. Then Hart accelerated the pace until he became the first Tribe general manager since Hank Greenberg to win a title.

But Hart never would have gained that distinction had he not made the sales job of his life to Jacobs. It began in 1991 when Hart and his assistant, Dan O'Dowd, were 30,000 feet above ground. As they sat in an airplane, they concocted a plan that changed the course of the franchise.

"We had just lost an arbitration case to Greg Swindell," Hart said. "I told Danny, 'We're never going through this again.' Swindell was a guy we pulled for every time he took the mound for us; then we had to go into a hearing and trash him just to try and keep his salary in line. Then it was being decided by someone (an arbitrator) who isn't even a baseball guy. The whole system made no sense. I can't tell you how much I hated the whole thing."

Swindell had a 12-9 record but an inflated 4.40 ERA. He was awarded $2 million by the arbitrator, putting his salary in the top 10 percent for all pitchers in 1991.

Disgusted by having someone else set their payroll, Hart and O'Dowd hatched what became a baseball revolution. They stared at the roster and targeted 12 players they wanted to be the core of their team. They planned to sign all 12 to multi-year contracts.

"We were trying to save a doomed franchise," Hart said. "Big-market teams were going to continue to blow us right out of the water. We'd continue to lose our best and brightest young players — either to free agency or be forced to trade them before they became free agents."

Hart and O'Dowd decided they'd pay their best prospects more than they were worth at that time with the hope that they would stay with the Indians for a little less tomorrow.

Before they could do that, Hart had to convince Jacobs to write the checks.

As Hart sat down with Jacobs, his throat was a little tight. He felt his heart beat just a bit faster and there was a slight shiver as a trace of cold sweat dripped down his back. Hart felt like a player before a big game.

"I had been general manager for less than a year (six months, actually)," Hart said. "And there I was, asking my owner to commit millions of dollars on a plan that had never been tried before."

Jacobs was 67 years old in 1992, a man who had made his millions in shopping malls such as the Galleria in downtown Cleveland and fast-food franchises such as Wendy's.

"I've never been afraid of taking risks," Jacobs said.

He did that when he bought the nearly bankrupt Indians in December of 1986 for $34 million. And here Hart was asking Jacobs to throw the dice again.

"I wanted Dick to go way out on a limb and head into the great unknown," Hart said. "If it blew up in my face, I'd probably never be a general manager again."

"John had his honor on the line," Jacobs said. "And I had my checkbook."

He listened to the then-43-year-old Hart speak with passion about his plan to sign young players to long-term contracts "so we can have a real good idea where our payroll will be one, two, three years from now."

Jacobs saw a bit of himself in his general manager. Hart was hustling, dreaming and scheming. It was the kind of vision that had made Jacobs one of the most powerful businessmen in the Midwest.

As Hart talked, Jacobs remembered when he was a 10-year-old kid in west Akron who had started mowing Wes Swenson's lawn. Jacobs' goal was to convince the fast-food restaurant owner that he would make a great carhop.

At 12, Jacobs got hired by Swenson to work in the basement of his restaurant peeling onions and potatoes. It was Jacobs' first real summer job.

"I wanted to get upstairs where I thought the action was," Jacobs said.

In the summer of his 13th year, Jacobs became a Swenson's carhop.

"I did that all the way through (Buchtel) high school," he said. "I could spot a Cadillac coming two blocks away, and I'd get my foot in front of the other guys and say, 'That car is mine,' because I knew the folks who drove those cars usually were better tippers."

Hart was proposing to use the same tactics — getting a leg up and getting to the players first. Jacobs gave Hart the green light and a long rope.

During a three-week stretch in spring training of 1992, Hart and O'Dowd signed 11 of their 12 players — the key ones being Sandy Alomar, Carlos Baerga and Charlie Nagy.

"We told the guys that we'd make a commitment to Cleveland together," Hart said. "We told them that maybe this wasn't the last dollar they could get, but it was a lot of money. These contracts (three to four years) gave them security, their family security and even their family's family security. We were paying them like established players even before they proved themselves."

The only miss was Albert Belle, who didn't like any of Hart's offers and wasn't sold on the long-range battle plan.

"That worried me," Hart said. "All the other guys were making $500,000 and driving new cars. We had to renew Albert's contract (at

$168,000) even though he had hit 28 homers the year before."

The signing of so many players for so many years, even though they had done so little in the major leagues, shocked much of baseball.

"I had good friends who were other general managers calling me and saying, 'John, I can't understand what you're doing. What if these guys get hurt? What if they can't play?' I asked myself those same questions, but we had to get some stability and build a team," Hart said. "Baseball people were floored. But if we hadn't signed those guys back then, we wouldn't be in the playoffs now."

Or, as Jacobs said: "Now you see most people in baseball trying to do what we did first."

In the spring of 1993, Albert Belle signed for three years plus an option in 1996. That was the same spring that Steve Olin and Tim Crews were killed in the boating accident.

The Indians finished with a 76-86 record for the second year in a row in 1993, but there was hope as the Tribe was moving into Jacobs Field in 1994. It was contention time, and it was Jacobs' move again.

Hart reminded Jacobs how they had cut the payroll by dealing off veterans such as Tom Candiotti, Joe Carter and Swindell. He told Jacobs: "It is time for us to step up to the plate and sign a couple of free agents."

He had two in mind — Dennis Martinez and Eddie Murray. Jacobs swallowed hard and reached for his checkbook as Hart again put his reputation on the line.

What if Martinez and Murray ended up like pitcher Wayne Garland and first baseman Keith Hernandez, the injured ghosts of past Tribe free-agent signings? The Indians were close to contending for the first time since 1959, but signing the wrong guys and wasting Jacobs' cash could kill their chances.

On Dec. 2, 1993, Jacobs committed $15 million to those veterans. That sent another shock wave through baseball: The Indians really were serious about winning.

"That was an expensive day," Jacobs said. "But these players had success and character. I wanted that to rub off on the young players. We also were in Jacobs Field, and I could make some projections on our revenue. That made it easier to move forward."

But Jacobs also did it because of his faith in Hart.

Hart says that a general manager's job is to build a contender and protect his owner's financial interests. Jacobs calls Hart "conservative" when it comes to spending. Hart continually updates his payroll projections and presents them to Jacobs. In the fall of 1995, Hart had numbers through the 1997 season.

Hart presented three free-agent plans to Jacobs before the start of the 1995 season: There was a $6 million package, another package for $3 million and a third for $1 million.

"We could have signed a Kevin Brown for $4.5 million like Baltimore did," Hart said. "But Dick suggested we try the $3 million, and it turned out to be the best approach. For $3 million, we got Orel Hershiser, Jim Poole, Paul Assenmacher and Dave Winfield. That really helped our team, and Dick deserves credit for spending the money and not just sitting tight."

Jacobs did prevent Hart from dealing for Bret Saberhagen. He brought up Saberhagen's contract, which has payments into the next century. He mentioned the pitcher's history of arm injuries.

"Dick didn't say, 'Don't do it.' We kept talking about it until I realized he was right," Hart said.

"I usually don't interfere in baseball judgments unless it is something as obvious as the nose on my face," Jacobs said. "And I have a pretty big nose."

Jacobs admires the fact that Hart has kept his family together — no easy task in the high-stakes world of sports business. John and Sandi Hart have been married for 24 years. Their daughter Shannon attends Cleveland State.

"You wouldn't believe the wonderful letters that Shannon has written over the years," Hart said. "I keep them in my desk drawer and I'll keep them forever."

A good husband and father, yes, but Hart's obsession is baseball.

"I don't take long vacations," he said. "I don't have barbecues in the back yard. I love tennis and golf, but I seldom have time to play. I love doing this job. I can't wait to wake up and go to the park. I love to be surrounded by people like Dan O'Dowd, (scouting director) Jay Robertson and (minor league director) Mark Shapiro — guys who share my same passions. Jay Robertson was on the road for 160 straight days scouting. That is the kind of dedication I'm talking about."

Then Hart discussed a guy named Jeff Datz, the Tribe's Class A manager at Columbus, Ga. But he also could have been talking about the John Hart of the mid 1980s.

"If Jeff gets on a bus after a long game, drinks six beers and then falls asleep, he shortchanges us," Hart said. "But I know that Jeff rides that bus all night and stares out the window at the moon over the Carolina mountains as he thinks about how to make Jaret Wright a better pitcher. He is doing the same job I'm doing here in Cleveland."

And he's doing it Hart's way.

15

And Speaking Of The Tribe

Oct. 1, 1995: The Indians won their 100th game of the season, beating the Kansas City Royals 17-7. It was only the second time in Tribe history that the team had won 100 games. The Indians did it in grand style — the 17 runs being their biggest explosion since May 4, 1991, ironically the year in which they lost 105 games. The Indians finished the season with a 100-44 record, winning the Central Division by 30 games, the widest margin by which any team has ever rolled to a title. In the Tribe radio booth, Herb Score and Tom Hamilton called the game. Score finished up his 32nd season behind the mike, and Hamilton completed his sixth.

Some of us wonder why Herb Score doesn't always call Indians games the way we see them. It could be because Herb Score has seen more Indians games than anyone — ever.

And he has seen the worst of the Indians — from Frank Lane to Beer Night to Gus Gil.

Score joined the team as a pitcher in 1955 and later returned as a broadcaster in 1964. In his first 31 years of Tribe play-by-play, only seven teams had winning records.

"It's safe to say that Herb Score has seen more bad baseball than anyone in the history of the game," said Joe Tait, one of Score's former broadcasting partners.

No wonder there were days when Score seemed as confused as the beleaguered boys on the field.

Herbisms have been as much a part of Tribe baseball as Cleveland

Stadium itself, and every Tribe fan has his favorite Score story.

Another former partner, the late Nev Chandler, was a wonderful mimic and often sounded more like Score than Herb did.

"One day I said that Cecil Cooper was batting 19-for-42 against the Tribe," Chandler recalled.

To which Score replied: "I am not good at math, but even I know that 19-for-42 is over .500."

Well, not exactly. But like the rest of us, Chandler let it pass. It was just Herb being Herb.

So were such Score comments as, "Swing and a miss, called strike three," or "There's a two-hopper to Vizquel, who catches it on the first bounce."

One day, Score interviewed veteran baseball writer Sheldon Ocker "from the Akron Beagle Journal." He meant the Beacon Journal, but every baseball season has its dog days and that was one for Score.

Those of us born after 1954 — after the last time the Indians won a pennant — think of Score as a broadcaster, not as a team member. Most of us have learned that Score once played, but few of us realize how well.

"He would have been a Hall of Famer," said Hank Peters, the former Tribe president. "He was Sandy Koufax before there was Sandy Koufax."

Score was a left-handed pitcher who won 36 games in his first two big-league seasons. He was 16-10 with a 2.85 earned-run average as the American League Rookie of the Year in 1955. The next season, he was 20-9 with a 2.53 ERA.

By the spring of 1957, Score was a two-time All-Star and he had twice led the league in strikeouts. The Indians turned down an offer of $1 million in cash from Boston for Score; that would be like $50 million today.

All this before his 24th birthday.

Score threw hard, worked harder, and was relentlessly polite to everyone. He and roommate Rocky Colavito were the most popular players on the team. But early in the 1957 season, a line drive by Yankee Gil McDougald hit Score in the eye. He missed most of the next two seasons. He pitched through 1963, but was never close to being the same pitcher.

"People talk about the eye accident," Score said. "That didn't ruin my career. I hurt my elbow right after I came back. That is what did it — a sore arm. Today, my eye is fine. My vision is close to 20-20."

Score seldom talks about his pitching days. When asked about them, he displays no bitterness and discusses his pitching in a matter-of-fact fashion, almost as if he's talking about someone else. Yet, he is a bright man — he knows how great he could have become. But he almost shrugs it off. A devout Catholic, Score says he believes that some things simply are out of his control, so why dwell on it?

"Herb is so patient with the fans," said Tom Hamilton, his current radio partner. "People will come up to him and say some really rude things about his eye accident. They probably don't mean it that way, but they come out bad. Herb just smiles and lets it roll off him. I really admire him for that."

While his pitching career was cut short, the longevity of Score the broadcaster is remarkable. He has a nasal, Long Island accent that can be a bit disconcerting unless you grew up listening to it.

Longtime listeners aren't surprised when Score launches into one of his dissertations about the weather. He will tell us more than we need to know about how the clouds look and how the wind blows as a storm forms over Lake Erie. If the Indians are playing in a dome, then Score will give the weather conditions both outside and in.

Score is not especially colorful, though fans are amused by his gaffes, such as the one during a 1995 American League playoff game, when he said the Indians were playing "Toronto," when they actually were in Seattle's Kingdome.

"I don't have any pet phrases," Score said. "Why say, 'Going, going, gone,' on a home run when the guy hits the ball out like a bullet? Then I just say, 'That ball is gone,' because it is."

So what is his secret to successful broadcasting?

"I like to talk to the fans as if they were at the game sitting next to me," Score said. "I let them know what happened, what interests me. I don't second-guess much, or try to manage the game. I broadcast it. I'd rather let the father tell his son that this is a good time in the game to bunt or pull the pitcher. The broadcaster doesn't have to be the expert on everything."

And the mistakes?

"Once it's out of your mouth, it's out of your mouth," Score said. "It's gone. I can't bring it back. I just correct it and move on."

Score doesn't listen to tapes of his broadcasts.

"I heard it once when I said it. Why do I need to hear it again?" he asked.

That is part of Score's charm. He is a nice guy who doesn't sweat the small stuff.

"A true gentleman" is how most of his friends characterize Score, who is known for his tireless charity work in the area.

Perhaps it comes down to this: Most Indians fans don't love Score the way Detroit loved Ernie Harwell, but they know Score and are comfortable with him.

Just as he is comfortable with the Tribe.

"What do I have to complain about?" Score asked. "I have the best job in baseball. I get to go to all the games, but I'm under none of the pressure. When the game is over, I can forget it and go home to my family."

Baseball is baseball to Herb Score. No matter if the game is one in the spring played by replacement players or an October playoff — it is all pretty much the same to Score.

"What's so hard about it?" he asked. "The pitcher throws ball one; I say, 'Ball one.' He throws ball two; I say, 'Ball two.' When someone hits the ball, I say where they hit it. I don't care if it's Little League, college, or the big leagues. It's still the game that we all can understand, and I'm paid to call the games, no matter who is playing."

Baseball may be just a game, but to Tom Hamilton it's a game with homework. He scours newspapers and magazines for information. He works the clubhouses before each game, gathering tidbits on both teams.

An upbeat, positive guy, Hamilton has always had tremendous respect for big-league baseball players.

"You won't hear me saying that these guys are stiffs," he said. "I hate it when someone uses that term to describe a professional baseball player. It's the cruelest word in sports. I wish I had the ability to play Class A ball and be called a stiff. Most of the people who call players stiffs usually are frustrated guys who were cut from their high school teams."

Hamilton and Score agree on this point: The Indians have never told them how to broadcast the games.

"In my six years doing the games, the Indians have never told me what to say or not say," Hamilton said. "(Owner) Dick Jacobs paid me after the (1994) strike, and with two children and a third on the way, my wife and I will always be grateful to Dick Jacobs and the Indians. All the Indians said is that they want me to be enthusiastic and positive. That comes easy for me since that's my nature. But you can't sugarcoat it. If a guy commits a bonehead play, I'll say that it's a bonehead play. In this business, your credibility is important."

Hamilton spent three years as the radio voice of the Class AAA Columbus Clippers before he was hired by the Tribe.

"To me, I have the best job in the world," he said. "When I was in the minors, I'd listen to Herb and the other big-league broadcasters on the radio and it seemed so removed — like I'd never get there. Now there are days when I'm doing the Indians games and I see myself sitting there next to Herb, and I really can't believe how lucky I've been."

And what does Hamilton think of that man he's sitting next to, that man who has spent 32 seasons as the voice of the Tribe?

"He is absolutely unflappable," Hamilton said. "Nothing fazes Herb. He is always telling me not to worry about things I can't control, and he really does live his life that way. I admire him for that."

A lot of people know Tom Hamilton the broadcaster, but there's another Tom Hamilton, too: Tom Hamilton the family man.

He can often be found playing ball with his son in the backyard of their Avon Lake home. Nicholas Hamilton will smack one of his dad's pitches and scream: "There's a swing and a drive to left . . . way back . . . it's gone!"

Then 5-year-old Nicholas will run around the bases. His father will smile and try to resist the urge to lift his son right off the ground — at least until Nicholas crosses home plate.

The fact that Nicholas imitates his father's famed home-run call isn't what makes Tom Hamilton smile. What makes Tom and Wendy Hamilton so proud is the fact that their son can still hear Indians broadcasts on the radio.

Hamilton will never forget Seattle, and not because it's a postcard city on Puget Sound or because that's where the Indians won the 1995 American League pennant. Seattle was where Hamilton was in 1993 when his wife called. She was in a doctor's office. She wanted to tell her husband what the doctor had found after examining Nicholas, but her throat was tight. There were no words. So the doctor said: "There is a chance that Nicholas will go deaf."

Hamilton couldn't believe it.

"Wendy first noticed that Nicholas didn't seem to be hearing well," Hamilton said. "We both started watching him more, and we noticed that he seemed to be sitting closer to the TV and that he just didn't seem to follow conversations like he did before."

Nicholas had been through a couple of ear infections, but he was 3½ years old back in 1993. Kids at that age always have ear infections. You take them to the doctor, the doctor drains the infection or gives the kid some medicine, and that's it — they're better. Kids don't go deaf, do they?

But the doctor was telling Hamilton that his son would hear only the sounds of silence.

"I kept thinking how unfair it was," he said. "They started talking about hearing aids, and I tried to think of any children who had hearing aids. I didn't know any."

Then Hamilton began to feel guilty. He wanted to be with his wife and his son. Instead, he was in a hotel room across the country.

"We'd been married for seven years," Wendy Hamilton said. "I consider Tom to be my best friend. We lean on each other a lot. But that night, all we could do was talk on the phone, and, really, all we did was cry. We had to do it long-distance, when what we really needed was to hold each other."

Both Hamiltons are religious and they found themselves making deals with God: "Dear Lord, you can take my left hand if you let Nicholas hear again . . . Lord, I'll do anything you ask, just tell me — just help Nicholas."

The exact nature of Nicholas' problem was unclear. Wendy and Tom combed their family histories, but could find no cases of hearing loss. Wendy went through videotapes of Nicholas as an infant and then as a toddler. She could tell his speech had changed and that it was getting worse.

"One day Nicholas told me, 'Mommy, my ears hurt,' and he held both his hands over his ears," Wendy Hamilton said. "We took him to the doctor right away, but I never expected to find out that he was losing 25 decibels of hearing a week."

By the time he was 4 years old, Nicholas' hearing loss already was moderate to severe. Furthermore, doctors were telling the Hamiltons, "There is nothing we can do."

"We kept asking ourselves how we could have missed it," Hamilton said. "And we wondered if we had caught it earlier, then maybe the doctors could have done something."

"It's like watching your child about to fall over a cliff, and you're a mile away and can't do a thing about it," Wendy Hamilton said.

But she wasn't ready to surrender.

"As we went to the various doctors and looked at the kids in the waiting room, they weren't like us," she said. "By that, I mean about every kid there had something genetic or a birth defect to explain their hearing loss."

The Hamiltons had planned to take a family vacation after the Indians finished their season in 1993.

"Instead, Wendy asked me if we should try to find a doctor to help

Nicholas," Hamilton said. "I was all for it. But she is the one who persisted and made all the calls."

Wendy Hamilton talked to more than a dozen specialists across the country before finding Dr. Charles Bluestone at Pittsburgh Children's Hospital. He gave them hope.

In the ear is a stirrup bone, and that bone wasn't fully formed in either of Nicholas' ears. The stirrup bone helps protect the inner ear. When Nicholas got an ear infection, there was nothing protecting the inside of the ear. The infection would drain into the inner ear, causing permanent damage.

Nicholas underwent two operations to build patches to protect the inner ear.

"It didn't reverse the damage," Wendy Hamilton said. "But it stopped any further damage."

These days Nicholas wears hearing aids. He attends speech class, although his speech is only slightly behind that of most 5-year-olds and shouldn't be a problem for long.

"Some children fight the hearing aids," Wendy said. "But Nicholas likes them because he wants to hear. But a while ago, I was driving with him next to me on Interstate 90. Suddenly, I heard this awful screech, and I knew that thing had just screamed right into his ear."

Wendy pulled the car over and helped Nicholas turn down the hearing aid. They both were in tears. He was scared. She was hurting for him.

"But given everything Nicholas has been through, we are so lucky," Wendy said. "He's a bright boy. Certain things bother him — wind blowing, conversations with a lot of people, or being in a place like a gym where there is an echo. But he is so happy and well-adjusted."

The Hamiltons also have two younger children. There is 3-year-old Kelsey, and the infant Bradley. They wanted several children and decided to continue to add to their family because the source of Nicholas' hearing problem remains a mystery.

"Obviously, we watch the kids' ears closely," Wendy said. "But so far, they've been fine."

Nicholas is doing well, too.

"There are times when things hit you," Hamilton said. "The other day, he was getting ready to start kindergarten, and he asked us if there would be boys and girls there with hearing aids, too."

It turned out that Nicholas was the only one in his class with hearing aids, but his classmates didn't care. Nicholas was just someone else to play with on the floor, another kid to chase around the playground.

While Nicholas won't be allowed to play football, he can play baseball, basketball and most other sports. He spends hours throwing a ball against the basement wall, catching it and making up imaginary baseball games.

"He is his dad's biggest fan," Wendy Hamilton said. "He listens to all the games, and when it's bedtime, he's always asking me to let him listen to the Indians bat once more."

Nicholas' hearing aid has four settings: Number 1 is the least powerful, Number 4 the most.

"When Albert Belle comes up, he turns it down to Number 1 because of the crowd noise," Wendy said. "When the other team is batting and it's quiet, he turns it up to Number 4. He has a good handle on things."

Especially on his father's voice.

"He loves to imitate me, especially my home-run call," Hamilton said. "I look at him and I just feel better. I wonder who am I to feel sorry for myself when Nicholas has never let it get him down."

16

THE DAY WE WAITED FOR

Mike Hargrove was worried as the Indians were preparing for their first post-season appearance in 41 years. Of course, for much of the 1995 season, Hargrove seemed to be having as much fun as a guy with hemorrhoids. He'd sit in the Indians dugout and sadly shake his head. He'd put both hands over his eyes, as if he didn't want to look. Remember, this was a man whose team was winning 100 games and sometimes he acted as if he'd just pulled into his driveway and discovered that his house had burned down.

"Just after you got through one type of pressure, there's another one," Hargrove said. "When we started the regular season and were about eight games up, I found myself thinking, 'Boy, I'd like to be ahead by about 12 games. Then I'd feel better.' We'd get up by 12 games, and I'd think, 'Well, 12 games is good, but I'd be more comfortable if we were up by about 18 games.' When we got up by 18 games, then everyone was saying how we had the division locked up."

But Hargrove had two words on his mind: Gene Mauch.

"I was thinking, 'We're up 18 games — man, I hope we don't blow this thing!' The pressure was even greater. I didn't want to be the Gene Mauch of Cleveland."

Mauch managed the 1964 Philadelphia Phillies, a team that blew a 6½-game lead with 13 games left in the season.

"Gene Mauch is a great baseball man," Hargrove said. "But every time someone mentions Gene Mauch's name, I'll guarantee you that people who know baseball say, 'Wasn't Mauch the guy who blew that six-game lead with the Phillies?' No one deserves that label, especially Gene. But it happens to you once, and they never let you forget it."

Hargrove didn't need to worry about becoming another Gene Mauch. His team won the American League's Central Division by a record 30 games.

"But as soon as we clinched, I started thinking about the playoffs," he said.

What if the Indians — the most dominating team during the regular 1995 season — didn't even make it to the World Series? What if they lost to Boston in the first round? What if the world ended?

Hargrove pondered all those questions.

"At the start of the season, I know a lot of people picked us to win the division, but I don't know how many people *really* believed it," he said. "I think they wanted us to win. Now that we have . . . I mean, I heard a guy call a talk show and say, 'If the Indians don't get to the World Series, it will be like the Browns and The Drive and all that. I will accept nothing less than a world championship.' I understand the mentality about wanting to win the World Series, but I'm not going to sit here and say, 'If we get beat in the first round of the playoffs, the season has been a failure.' This has been a tremendous season, and nothing can take that away from us."

Hargrove knew he was on the spot, especially in the first round of the playoffs. His team was so overpowering, that it was assumed that a botched managing job would be the only way the Indians could lose. All the manager had to do was push the right buttons.

"There are no push-button managers," Hargrove said. "This team's consistency has been tremendous, and I think the managers and coaching staff have had something to do with that."

Hargrove was in a contemplative mood as his team prepared to face the Eastern Division champion Boston Red Sox. His team was a collection of high-strung and sometimes moody folks who weren't always thrilled to hear the voice of authority.

"On a minor league team, the manager can say, 'Fellows, this is the way it's going to be done, and if you don't like it, we'll find someone else to take your place and you can go home,' " Hargrove said. "You can't do that with Albert Belle. You can't tell that to Carlos Baerga, Dennis Martinez, Kenny Lofton or Eddie Murray. There are *no* other people to take their places, and they know it. So you have to find different ways to make them understand the benefit of doing something *this* way instead of *that* way. It can be a difficult thing to do. It can take a day, a week, sometimes even more than a year. That is how teams grow."

And growth — maturity — was the key to the Indians' success in 1995.

"I haven't had a meeting all year where I had to rant and rave, scream and throw things," he said. "There were days when I wanted to, but it never seemed like the right time. Then the guys bounced back. We have a lot of veteran leadership on this team, and they have really made my job easier."

Those veteran players were about to help Hargrove against Boston, but he didn't know it then. He had to wait to see it.

The Oct. 3 opener of the best-of-five series with Boston was at Jacobs Field. That day it rained — all day. There were thunderstorms in the afternoon and then showers. The game was supposed to start at 8 p.m., and it was still raining.

Maybe that's what happens when two teams are cursed.

The Indians and their fans had been waiting 41 years for this night. Forty-one years of bad trades, bungled management and personal tragedies.

As for the Red Sox, well, Boston hadn't won a World Series since 1918.

And so, it rained.

Finally, the rain diminished to a drizzle and the game began — 39 minutes late.

It was not a good omen for the Indians. The Indians won 27 games in their last at-bat in 1995. They were 13-0 in extra innings during the regular season; they were 74-5 when they were ahead after six innings. But here's a statistic they don't talk about: The Indians were only 5-6 in games delayed by rain.

After six innings in this first playoff game, the Indians had a 3-2 lead, thanks to a run-scoring single by Eddie Murray. Remember, the Indians were 74-5 when they led after six innings.

But they couldn't hold the lead this time and the game plowed on. Through the rain.

Boston tied the game in the top of the eighth, and it remained 3-3 heading into the 11th inning.

Then, Indians pitcher Jim Poole, carrying 41 years of hopes and frustrations in his left hand, coughed up a home run to Tim Naehring, and Boston took a 4-3 lead into the bottom of the 11th.

But the game wasn't over. Albert Belle (Who else?) hit a home run off Rick Aguilera, ace of the Red Sox bullpen and a guy with 32 saves in 1995. Once again the score was tied.

Clearly, Boston Manager Kevin Kennedy had been waiting for a moment like this.

Earlier in the game, Belle had hammered two runs in with a double to left field. Now, as a tightly wound Belle rounded the bases, Kennedy bounced out of the dugout and asked home-plate umpire Tim Welke to confiscate Belle's bat. Welke complied, and Belle's bat was taken into the umpires' room at Jacobs Field.

Does this sound familiar? Remember 1994 and the Chicago White Sox series in late July? Belle was a one-man wrecking crew until Chicago Manager Gene Lamont asked the umpires to check Belle's bat for cork.

That bat was taken to the umpires' room and then one of the Indians broke into the room and stole it, replacing it with a Paul Sorrento model. The switch didn't fool anyone and the Indians were then accused of cheating and stealing, compounding the felony. Eventually a Belle bat was turned over, and x-rays showed it was full of cork. Belle was suspended for seven games.

Strangely, throughout the 1995 season, no one asked to have Belle's bat checked. But now it was playoff time and Kennedy was demanding that the bat be checked.

Hargrove rushed onto the field to scream at the umpires and to hurl some unrepeatable words at the Boston manager. In the dugout, Belle made a muscle and pointed to his biceps. "It's my muscles, man," he yelled at the Red Sox.

At Jacobs Field, a fan had hung this sign: "CHIEF WAHOO IS MY LIFE." So it seemed in northeast Ohio that rainy October night. The game dragged on past midnight, past 1 in the morning. No one dared go to sleep, or even leave the TV set for a moment.

Finally, at 2:08 a.m. Oct. 4, 1995, the Indians won their first post-season game since 1948. They won it because of Tony Pena, the Tribe's back-up catcher, a guy who wasn't even supposed to be in the game.

Sandy Alomar started behind the plate, but he was playing with a bulky brace on his left knee — a knee that had undergone surgery twice in 10 months. In the 10th inning, Alomar surprised the Red Sox by bunting for a hit. He hobbled to first, beating the throw.

Hargrove knew that Alomar represented the winning run and that because of his knee he'd need a taxi to get around the bases. So Hargrove put Wayne Kirby in as a pinch runner. But the Indians couldn't drive Kirby home, and Pena went behind the plate to replace Alomar.

Pena came to bat with two outs in the bottom of the 13th inning. Zane Smith, who was pitching for Boston, missed the strike zone with his first three pitches. Pena stepped out of the batter's box and stared at third base coach Jeff Newman.

The count was three balls and no strikes. Pena wondered if he was supposed to swing or take a pitch in the hope of drawing a walk.

Newman gave a sign. Pena nodded. Smith delivered a fastball and Pena swung.

In the dugout, Hargrove wondered: What was Tony doing?

Then he saw where the ball was going. As Indians radio announcer Tom Hamilton likes to say, "There's a drive, deep to left . . . way back . . . *it's gone!*"

The ball landed in the first row of the left-field bleachers. The 38-year-old Pena ran around the bases with his arms above his head. He looked like a little kid who had just won a T-ball game with a hit.

Pena was mobbed at the plate. He was laughing, but there were tears in his eyes. The Indians had won, 5-4.

Did Pena have a green light to swing at that 3-0 pitch?

"Well, you could say it was amber," Hargrove said.

Actually, the light was red, but Pena was so excited he failed to read the correct sign from Newman. A veteran who should have known better made a mental mistake — and hammered the ball out of the park to win a game in the 13th inning.

Pena is known for swinging at bad pitches. His mother lives in the Dominican Republic. She was a star softball player and she taught her son how to play ball. She watches Indians games on satellite TV. Each week she calls and criticizes Pena, telling him to take more pitches, to be patient at the plate.

"Ma, you're right," Pena tells her. "I swing too much."

But 1995 was an Indians summer — a time when everything seemed to come out right for those wearing a Cleveland uniform. A batter gets his signals mixed up, and what happens? The Indians win their first playoff game.

Meanwhile, in Boston, the fans were saying: "Tony Pena? I mean, *Tony Pena!* When the guy played for us, he couldn't even hit a fair ball."

So the Red Sox were cursed by a guy who had once been one of their own.

You would think that by 3 in the morning people would be going home. Instead, this was the hour for surgery on Belle's bat.

Immediately after the Indians' victory, General Manager John Hart went into the bowels of Jacobs Field in an attempt to save the bat.

"I wanted to tell Dr. Bobby Brown (the American League consultant) that he could take the bat over to Lutheran Medical Center and get it x-rayed," Hart said. "But five to 10 minutes after the game, I got down there and they had already sawed it in half."

Brown is a cardiologist and he didn't think it was a good idea to walk into a hospital emergency ward at 3 a.m. and ask technicians to x-ray a bat. "They have better things to do," Brown said.

So a saw was found and the surgery was performed. The bat was clean. No cork this time.

The Indians were hot.

"Albert's bat never should have been sawed in half," Hart said. "That is the bat that he broke the team home-run record with. (Al Rosen's old mark was 43 in 1953.) It's also the bat with which Albert hit his 50th home run. It was a very special bat to him."

Hart called American League president Gene Budig to tell him that and more.

"Dr. Brown said he did it right away so he could get word to the media," Hart said. "But he never did. He just took a hike and the American League put out a statement saying that it was still investigating the matter. That really upset me."

Hart, Hargrove and the players also were furious with the Red Sox.

"OK, the Red Sox wanted to check Albert's bat; that is their right," Hart said. "Mike Hargrove and I don't play the game that way, but if they want to, well, that's their business. We wouldn't pull something like that, but maybe we're not as smart as the Red Sox. All I know is that the league could have handled it better."

A few times during 1995, the Indians were told that other teams might start checking bats because the team was having such an overpowering season.

"I knew Albert's bat was clean and I know our team is clean," Hart said. "We talked to our players about it during spring training. We told them that because of what happened last season (Belle's suspension), some teams might try to disrupt and distract us (by checking bats)."

The Red Sox acted sheepish about exactly who had ordered them to have the bat checked.

Catcher Bill Haselman said Manager Kevin Kennedy told him to do it.

Kennedy mumbled about having "certain information" about the bat. He hinted that Some Players Who Knew Other Players had whispered that Belle was cheating.

"I think they ended up looking a little foolish," Hart said. "No one had checked our bats all year. The only bat that was checked this season was when (Yankees Manager) Buck Showalter asked the umpires to look at (California's) Tony Phillips' bat. It was clean."

Hart saw the heavy hand of Boston General Manager Dan Duquette behind the bat caper.

"I heard an interview where he said that Albert hit 50 homers, and no one else had much over 40," Hart said. "He indicated that there was something fishy about all of Albert's power. Well, look at last year: Albert was ready to hit close to 50 if the strike hadn't gotten in his way."

Of course, the Red Sox could have countered with the fact that Belle was caught with a corked bat in 1994.

Though Belle did lose his bat — and one that was special to him — the playoff controversy did some good. That sawed-in-half clean bat restored Belle's integrity.

"The incident also brought our team together," Hargrove said.

Just as Hart had little respect for Boston General Manager Dan Duquette, Hargrove was no fan of Boston Manager Kevin Kennedy. He refused to shake Kennedy's hand before the start of the second playoff game.

Hargrove and Kennedy had managed against each other in the Class AAA Pacific Coast League in 1989. Kennedy's Albuquerque team had beaten Hargrove's Colorado Springs team in the playoffs, and Kennedy liked to remind Hargrove of that by recounting the story to reporters.

As Game 2 was about to begin at Jacobs Field, Albert Belle's face was on the scoreboard. Belle held up his arm, made a muscle, and pointed to his biceps — a reference to the bat incident.

A record crowd of 44,264 fans, a sea of red, white and blue, stood and roared. It was an ovation for nothing more than a picture on the Jumbotron.

The first round of the American League playoffs was, for all intents and purposes, over when Tony Pena rounded the bases at 2:08 that Oct. 4 morning.

Yes, the Indians had two more games to win, but the Red Sox never had a chance.

The Indians really didn't need Albert Belle or his bat to beat Boston 4-0 in Game 2, as Orel Hershiser was brilliant. With a little help from the bullpen, the Indians were winners.

Game 3 was in Fenway Park, and the Tribe blasted Boston, 8-2.

As the Indians were wrapping up the series, I couldn't help but think: Somewhere, Rocky Colavito was smiling. So were Andre Thornton, Leon Wagner, Duane Kuiper and all the other good guys who ever did time in the stalag known as Indians baseball.

Those guys all wanted to play on a team like this, a team that now must be considered one for the ages — at least by those of us too young to remember 1948 or 1954.

This third playoff game was for the fans, whose fathers or mothers took us by the hand down the West Third Street bridge and into that old, cold, empty Cleveland Stadium. We ate bad hot dogs and good mustard. We drank flat Cokes, the fizz seemingly sapped out of them just like it had been zapped from the team. For 35 years, we watched a team that was the most futile, depressing and cursed in all of baseball.

We all had our heroes, of course — players who seemed to struggle mightily against a tide they knew would draw them under. For some, it was Gaylord Perry, who at least made the hapless Indians of the early 1970s a great team every fourth day when he pitched. For others, it was Thornton, who would have hit 40 homers a year if he had been protected in a decent lineup. Sometimes the hero was the one Indians ballplayer who simply took the time to sign a young fan's scorecard or shake his hand.

Most of our Indians memories were good, even if the teams were terrible.

How can any of us who grew up with Jack Kralick, Jack Brohamer or Super Joe Charboneau do anything but stare in awe at the 1995 Indians, who swept Boston in the best-of-five playoff series?

In the past there had been Indians teams that had given us a glimmer of hope, but then the Yankees would show up for a four-game series over the Fourth of July weekend and tne season would be finished after the promotional fireworks. Then, Indians owner/general manager Gabe Paul would mumble something about how "the team hasn't jelled yet."

Paul also told us that "Cleveland was a sleeping giant," but he neglected to tell us that the team was auditioning for a remake of Rip Van Winkle.

For all those years we had been told that the Indians would get better. And we never believed it. Not until this night in Fenway Park.

The Indians of 1995 just turned up the volume on their clubhouse stereos and kept on winning. They won 100 games in the regular season and lost only 44.

The deck was stacked against them in baseball's ridiculous new playoff system, which denied the team with the best regular-season record the home-field advantage. Their response: "So what?"

"We've waited 41 years for this, and we'll play in St. Petersburg, Russia, if that's what it takes," said Manager Mike Hargrove.

These Indians should have faced the wild card team, but didn't. They should have had the home-field advantage, but didn't. And it didn't matter. They won their two games at Jacobs Field and went on to Boston. There could have been three games in Fenway, but they took the Sox out early.

As I watched the Indians put away the Red Sox, I kept thinking: This team wins because it expects to win. It has talent and swagger. It is a team for a new generation of Tribe fans, for kids who one day will look back at 1995 and realize how lucky they were to have watched a team we older fans never dared dream we'd see.

In the Tribe dressing room after that third playoff victory, the mood was pleased but subdued.

It could have been another day in July, another game and another win. No one was jumping up and down on the field. No champagne corks were popping in the clubhouse. There were lots of smiles and a little laughter.

The team's theme song, *That's The Way We Do It*, blared on the stereo system. But it's always on after the Indians win.

"We are happy that we've won," said Orel Hershiser, "but it is sort of like, 'What did we win?' I mean, we still have to play another American League team before we get to the World Series. This whole playoff system is an odd sequence of events. The mood in here is that we're happy we've won the game, but we really haven't won anything yet."

17

IN THE LION'S MOUTH

Who would have guessed that it would be the Seattle Mariners who would stand in the way of the Indians making their first trip to the World Series in 41 years?

Seattle? Come on.

The Mariners were the Tribe-West — only they hadn't been around as long. The Seattle franchise had been in existence for 19 years and never had won a thing. The Mariners were exactly like the Indians after The Curse of Colavito — no contention, no hope, not much of anything to cheer about.

It was even like that for the Mariners for most of 1995. Then they got hot. They beat the California Angels in a one-game playoff to win the Western Division title.

In the first round of the playoffs, Seattle lost its first two games to the Yankees, and everyone assumed the Indians would be in New York to open the American League Championship Series. But the Mariners returned home and took three in a row from New York.

Before most Tribe fans could find Seattle on their maps, the Indians were on a charter flight to Washington to open a seven-game series against the Mariners.

"This whole thing scares the hell out of me," said John Hart.

He meant the playoffs, and he especially meant playing Seattle.

"I hate the dome," he said. "Ever since I have been with the Indians, terrible things have happened to us in the dome."

Hart has Seattle stories — terrible Tribe tales of games lost that were won . . . of Carlos Baerga making two errors in the ninth inning . . . of Doug Jones blowing a three-run lead in the ninth . . . of crazy hops off the artificial turf that turned outs into hits.

Hart talked about Seattle's Kingdome as if it were the Devil's Island of baseball. But he was downright passive about the place compared to

Rick Manning.

"If it were up to me, I'd blow it up and never think twice," said the Tribe's TV broadcaster.

Manning played center field for the Indians from 1975 to 1983. He remembered when the Indians were the Indians, the Mariners were the Mariners, and most fans could care less about either team — they both stunk.

"We'd come in here and there would be maybe 7,500 fans," Manning said. "This place is dead, gray. Look at the ceiling, the drab colors. I mean, you'd be outside and it was gray and raining, and you'd come inside and it would still be gray. Playing center field was like standing in the middle of a big warehouse."

There was one advantage to the small crowds.

"You could hear the vendors," Manning said. "There was the guy who sold peanuts, and he'd throw the bags behind his back. I'd hear that guy all over the park, and he was pretty entertaining."

Manning paused for a moment and then really spoke his mind.

"I just detest this place," he said, almost spitting the words. "In 1977, I beat out a bunt, then I tried to steal second. I did a normal slide into second base, but they kept the dirt area around the base too moist. I slid wrong and I ended up with a broken back. That changed my whole career, and I always remember that when I walk into this place."

Manning was a .290 hitter before the injury and closer to .250 afterwards. He played the outfield as well as ever, but never had the same spark or speed at the plate and on the bases. Whether the cause was physical, mental or a combination of the two, Manning was never the same after his back injury in Seattle.

One of Manning's Tribe teammates was Mike Hargrove, who loathes domes. He talks about domes "distorting the game." He especially hates the Kingdome, because the Indians always played so poorly there and because so few fans bothered to show up. He can work himself into such a state talking about the Kingdome that he can't even speak — he just bites his lower lip and seethes.

"The only time I remember this place full was the year they had Beach Towel Day," Hargrove said. "I came to bat, and they started doing the wave with 50,000 people waving beach towels in this dome. It was a very strange sight."

When the Indians opened the American League Championship Series in Seattle, it was like every game was Beach Towel Day. The town was in love with its baseball team — for the first time in 19 years — and there is nothing quite as vivid and intense as a first love. Seattle fans gave the Mariners standing ovations simply for stepping on the field during warm-ups.

For at least one person, this was a fantasy matchup. Randy Adamack is the Mariners' vice president of communications. You think selling Indians baseball was tough a job in the last 35 years? Think about what selling Mariners baseball was like. At least Cleveland had had a baseball team for as long as anyone could remember.

Adamack was born in Conneaut, Ohio, grew up a Tribe fan, and worked for the Indians from 1974 to 1978 as the team's public relations director. Then he moved to Seattle and has been there ever since.

"I was 3 years old when the Indians won the 1954 pennant," Adamack said. "I don't remember it, but for my whole life I heard stories about the 1948 Indians, the 1954 team, and players like Bob Feller, Bob Lemon and Lou Boudreau. There was a sense of history about the team. People's parents and grandparents always read about the Indians, listened to the team on the radio and talked about them."

Things were different when Adamack got to Seattle.

"When it came to baseball, there was no tradition," he said. "The Seattle Pilots were here in 1969 and left (for Milwaukee) after one year with a lot of ill will in the community (because of debts and the decision to leave). So their one experience with baseball here was very bad."

Since Adamack began working in baseball in 1974, only three of his teams have had a winning record.

"And there was never a pennant race until this year," he said. "I mean, people say that Seattle isn't a baseball town, but I never thought that was a fair statement. They had no baseball tradition before the Mariners, and then when the Mariners did start to play, they didn't win. It wasn't just the dome; it was the team. The truth is that for a long time there just wasn't much for the fans to get excited about."

The Mariners came into existence in 1977, and in the next 18 years their best record was 83-79 in 1991. In 1994, they were 49-63 before the strike mercifully ended their season.

"But the strike really hurt us in the off-season," Adamack said. "We had worked hard to get our season-ticket base up to 10,000. Then it dropped to 7,500 this year. Our group sales were down 50 percent. Then we started so-so. Heading into August, we were averaging about 18,000 fans, which was down from about 25,000 the previous two seasons."

Fans mumbled about the Kingdome being cold and impersonal — until the Mariners got hot and made it warm, fuzzy and a great place to yell until your throat turned raw.

"Seattle is like Cleveland in that I always thought it could be like this if the team was good," Adamack said. "But I never had any idea that it would happen to both teams in the same year."

I agreed with Adamack. I wanted the Indians to play Seattle, partly because no one else did.

That was especially true of television. The TV boys were thinking: *Cleveland? Seattle?* Who lives there? Do they have indoor plumbing yet? They wanted George Steinbrenner and Don Mattingly. They wanted New York because they all live in New York and believe the center of the universe is New York. To those who decide what we watch on television, Cleveland is a cow town and Seattle is somewhere north of Canada.

So what if Ken Griffey Jr. and Albert Belle were the two biggest stars in the American League?

So what if Randy Johnson was the most dominant pitcher we have? So what if he'd be facing a "lineup for the ages," as Orel Hershiser calls the Tribe batsmen?

So what if the Mariners deserved to go? They didn't back in through the wild card system. Under the old two-division setup, the Indians would have won the East, the Mariners the West, and they would have butted heads for the American League Championship.

So what if the Indians and Mariners would be the best series? So what if these two young teams were exactly what the game needed to heal some of the wounds of the strike?

The TV boys didn't care. They wanted New York.

Well, they could have New York. They could have druggies like Steve Howe and Darryl Strawberry. They could have hired guns like David Cone and Jack McDowell. They certainly could have the oafish Steinbrenner.

I knew that there were scores to be settled between the Indians and the Yankees. I knew that an entire generation of baseball fans grew up loathing the Yankees and everything for which they stood. If the Yankees had beaten the Mariners, it would have been some twisted form of baseball entitlement. They were a talented but underachieving team that didn't play well for most of the season, and only in this age of mediocre baseball could the 1995 Yankees be considered a team worthy of the post-season.

As the Indians were getting ready for Game 1 in Seattle, I just kept thinking: This would be fun. The network TV guys would be all confused (and so would poor Herb Score) with three guys named Martinez — Dennis, Tino and Edgar. Both teams had an abundance of Latin American stars, and the TV boys wouldn't like that because the Latin players tend to get nervous when interviewed on camera and their English suffers. Well, I've got news for any TV type who whines about the English spoken by most Latin players: You can bet their English is better than your Spanish.

Latin players are becoming the heart of baseball. In the United States, there is a raging debate about whether baseball is the Number 1 sport. In Latin America, there is no other sport.

When I first began covering baseball in the late 1970s, Latin players suffered from the same stereotypes that were pasted on the early black players. Latin players were supposed to be talented but moody, naturally gifted but fundamental disasters. They were said to play the game well while playing it all wrong — at least according to the American book of baseball.

But the Latin players have put their own translation and stamp on the game. They play baseball from the moment they can walk, much as children did in this country until the 1960s, when they discovered other sports such as basketball, football, golf, tennis and soccer.

Today's Latin players seem to be the most passionate about baseball. They are the ones who usually spend the most time with the writers and fans. Perhaps it is because they came from poverty the likes of which most of us can't imagine. They aren't as spoiled and jaded as their American counterparts, who often were pampered from the time they first touched a baseball bat. The Latin players are (for the most part) a bunch of nice guys who know they have great jobs. They are not formally educated, because most of them signed contracts when they were about 16 — before they could even finish high school in their native countries.

Carlos Baerga wanted to sign with the San Diego Padres when he was 15. His father, who worked in a bank in Puerto Rico, told Carlos to at least wait another year. Then, when he was 16, the Padres offered him $30,000 and Carlos was allowed to play ball. Where else could he make that kind of money?

Omar Vizquel left Caracas, Venezuela, at the age of 16 and began his pro career in Butte, Mont. Talk about culture shock! Going from Venezuela to Montana is like boarding a spaceship and getting off on Mars.

Julian Tavarez was 18 when he left the Dominican Republic and came to the United States, beginning his pro career with the Tribe's farm team in Burlington, N.C. During that first season in 1992, all he ate was fried chicken — even for breakfast. That was the only English he knew — other than baseball cuss words — so chicken was what he ate.

I thought about the Latin players when the Indians were about to face the Mariners. Here were all these guys from the Dominican Republic, Puerto Rico and Venezuela and they were playing for teams representing Seattle and Cleveland. And the game was being played in a dome near the Canadian border.

After the first game of the series, I knew why Hart hated the Kingdome.

The Indians had just lost the opener, 3-2. They lost to a pitcher named Bob Wolcott, who was 22 years old and the top prospect in the Seattle farm system. Wolcott had been in the majors for only six weeks. He started because Seattle Manager Lou Piniella was out of pitchers; he burned them all up in the five-game, first-round series with the Yankees.

This kid Wolcott walked the bases loaded to start the game, and the Indians didn't score.

Dennis Martinez started for the Tribe — 40-year-old Dennis Martinez who lives for this game — and the Indians didn't win.

During the last inning of the game, Martinez sat in the Kingdome dugout with a towel wrapped around his jaw and over his head. He looked like he had the world's worst toothache, which was exactly how he felt. He looked like his last friend in the world had just been carjacked by terrorists, which was how Tribe fans also were going to feel if the Indians lost the series.

The Indians were cursing the dome. They had just been beaten by a rookie pitcher and by a team whose mascot was a moose. And moose weren't exactly the Rhodes scholars of the animal kingdom. A week before the Indians arrived, the Mariner Moose went roller-blading after the fifth inning of a Seattle-New York game and crashed into the center-field wall, breaking an ankle. So the Mariners imported a fill-in Moose. This was the original Moose, who had quit in 1993 to pursue a singing career. All that singing had added 20 pounds, and it was a real chore to fit him into his old moose suit.

So the Indians lost to a kid pitcher and an old, fat moose.

That was why Hart was in absolute agony when I saw him the next day. It was about 8 in the morning, and we were both in the workout room of the Red Lion Hotel. Hart was on the Stairmaster for about 40 minutes.

He steamed and sweated as he watched ESPN, which showed clips of the Indians losing to Seattle — over and over and over. As Albert Belle swung at a pitch in the dirt to kill a rally, Hart said, "Go ahead, punish me some more."

Indians fans felt the same way.

"We are so close," Hart said. "We have played well all year. Now all we have to do is play well for another week."

Hart talked and talked about how the Indians would "be just fine." He talked about how "Orel will give us a great performance (in Game 2)." He talked about how the Indians really didn't hit that well in the Boston series, and the bats were due to break out. He kept assuring himself that everything would be fine.

Then he dropped to the floor and began doing push-ups.

"I didn't sleep at all last night," he said. "Not one wink. I just kept replaying the game over and over in my head."

Like a lot of Tribe fans, Hart was torturing himself, creating scenarios in which the Indians would come up just short of the World Series.

"You know, we deserve to be there," he said. "We just have to get there."

It was Orel Hershiser who eased the pain — for Mike Hargrove, for John Hart and for Indians fans.

If Hershiser was nervous pitching in the playoffs in front of 57,000 maniacs in the Kingdome, he didn't show it. In fact, he talked about how the roar of the crowd sounded like "the rolling waves of the ocean."

Dennis Martinez heard Hershiser say that and shook his head. "Orel must be smarter than me," he said. "When I hear people yelling, it's people yelling. He hears the ocean."

And he pitches like a captain who knows how to bring home the ship in stormy seas. Hershiser says that the key to pitching in October "isn't anything special. Big-game players tend to play the same in big games as they do normally, and maybe the pressure on the other players makes them go backwards. So that makes it look like you rose to the occasion, when all you really did was the same thing."

Hershiser has theories on everything, and he always seems to be trying out new ones.

Well, in Game 2 he was better than normal. He was great. He didn't know it at the time, but he probably saved the series for the Tribe.

The playoffs are Hershiser's stage, his time of year. Until Hershiser arrived on the scene in 1995, the Indians never had a Mr. October. The only Mr. October they had needed was the guy who had to hose down the old dressing rooms at the Stadium to wash out the stench of the previous season. Hershiser didn't worry about the Indians' trail-of-tears history. He didn't care. He came from Los Angeles, where October is when baseball begins.

He came to Cleveland with a 4-0 record in the post-season. After beating Boston in the first round of the playoffs and then Seattle in Game 2 of the second round, he was 6-0. In those 15 October innings for the Indians, he allowed one run. He didn't just beat Seattle, 5-2. He didn't just tie the best-of-seven series at 1-1. He returned order to the universe that was Cleveland Indians Baseball 1995.

"If we had lost this game and gone down 0-2 with Randy Johnson coming at us in Game 3," Hargrove said, and his voice dropped to a whisper and then reached a sudden stop. He didn't have to finish that frightening thought.

Hershiser proved that the man on the mound in the Kingdome was the most important man in the building. And he had all the emotion of an undertaker. He carved up the hottest team in baseball as if it were a slab of beef on his plate.

There were sinkers low and away — sinkers that Hargrove called "as close as you'll ever see to an unhittable pitch." One of those also was uncatchable. He whiffed Vince Coleman, but Coleman reached first base when the ball eluded catcher Sandy Alomar's mitt.

When the Seattle hitters decided to move in on home plate and take away that sinker, no problem. The Grim Reaper, as Hargrove calls Hershiser, just knocked the Mariners' butts down. He dusted them with hard stuff under the chin or made them dance with a fastball at the knees — as in a fastball that nearly took off the kneecap.

Hershiser was sending a message to the crazed converts to Seattle baseball. The Kingdome might be the Mariners' home, but home plate belonged to him. You want to stomp? You want to scream and wave your arms? You want to try and blow the roof off this joint? Hershiser gave you the feeling that he didn't even hear it.

He just heard the ocean. In stressful moments, he sang a Christian hymn to himself. What Hershiser did was show the Indians exactly what post-season baseball was all about.

The Seattle series was scary. It was nothing like the first round, the sweep over Boston. In that series, the Tribe needed 13 innings to beat the Red Sox in the opener, and then it was just a matter of time — Boston was done. Tony Pena's homer was enough to convince the Red Sox that Boston's Curse of the Bambino (Bambino as in Babe Ruth, whom the Sox traded away) was stronger than any Cleveland Curse of Colavito.

The Mariners were different. They came to Jacobs Field for Game 3 and beat the Indians in 11 innings. The final score was 5-2, but more important was the fact that this was the first time in 15 games that the Tribe had lost in extra innings.

That set up Game 4 at Jacobs Field on a chilly Saturday evening. Now it was up to a trade made by John Hart in late July to save the Indians.

On July 27, 1995, the Central Division pennant race was all but over; the Tribe already had a 15½-game lead. That's when Ken Hill came to town in the only significant deal engineered by the Indians during the regular season. Hill brought with him a 6-7 record and a 5.06 ERA; his ego (and best pitches) had been battered after two months in St. Louis.

"That trade was made with the post-season in mind," said Dan O'Dowd, the Indians' assistant general manager. "In July, we were already thinking about our starting rotation for the playoffs, and we knew that we needed one more experienced arm."

So Hart and O'Dowd went shopping.

The Chicago White Sox had Jim Abbott on the market, and the lefty looked like a perfect addition to a staff with no southpaws. But Chicago's asking price was Richie Sexson, Bartolo Colon and Alan Embree.

Hart and O'Dowd almost ate the telephone when they heard that. Colon (with a 13-3 record and 1.96 ERA) and Sexson (with a .306 batting average, 22 home runs and 85 RBI) played at Class A Kinston and were considered the two best young prospects in the Tribe farm system. Embree was ranked as the team's prime prospect as a left-handed reliever.

"No way we'd do that," O'Dowd said.

Toronto was dangling Cy Young award winner David Cone (who ended up in New York), but wanted pitcher Albie Lopez, Sexson and Maximo De La Rosa, another promising pitching prospect at Kinston.

"We went through 10 years of trades of this type, where you give up young players for a pitcher to get you over the top," O'Dowd said. "Most of them don't work. Some of them have been complete disasters."

In 1987, the Tigers swapped a young pitcher named John Smoltz for veteran Doyle Alexander. The immediate advantage was huge in favor of the Tigers, as Alexander won 10 in a row to help Detroit take the pennant.

But Alexander is long retired, and Smoltz started for the Atlanta Braves in the 1995 World Series.

"You really have to be careful," O'Dowd said.

Seattle ace Randy Johnson was the product of that kind of deal. The Mariners had a veteran lefty named Mark Langston, who was headed for free agency at the end of the 1989 season. The Expos thought they could win the pennant with one more pitcher, so Montreal traded three young arms for Langston. One of them was 6-foot-10 Randall David Johnson. The Expos withered on the vine in the 1989 pennant race, and Langston did not re-sign with them and moved on to California.

"We knew all the pitfalls," O'Dowd said. "When teams asked for guys like Colon and Sexson, we just weren't going to trade them."

Finally, the Indians looked to St. Louis and Hill, a 16-game winner for Montreal in 1994 and runner-up to Atlanta's Greg Maddux for that year's National League Cy Young Award. Montreal couldn't meet Hill's salary demands, so in the spring of 1995 he was traded to St. Louis, where he signed a one-year, $4.3 million contract. And then the athletic right-hander forgot how to pitch.

"A lot of teams backed off Hill because his mechanics were a mess," O'Dowd said. "He went from throwing about 93 mph last year down to the middle 80s. John (Hart) always liked Hill, and we decided to get him if the price wasn't too high."

The Cardinals were an embarrassment in 1995, and Hill was being hammered there. He would be a free agent at the end of 1995, and St. Louis had no interest in bringing him back. So the Indians traded three minor leaguers — infielder David Bell, pitcher Rick Heiserman and catcher Pepe McNeal — for the 29-year-old Hill.

"We really like David Bell, but we have Jimmy Thome at third and Carlos Baerga at second base," O'Dowd said. "There wasn't room for him, unless it was as a utility player. We gave up some decent prospects, but not the best in our farm system."

The first thing the Indians did was introduce Hill to pitching coach Mark Wiley, and the two of them began watching tapes of Hill in Montreal — it was the 1994-model Hill that the Indians needed in the playoffs.

"We knew that Kenny couldn't help us right after the deal," O'Dowd said. "We were strictly thinking about the playoffs."

During the regular season, Hill was a respectable 4-1 with a 3.98 ERA for Tribe. But more important, he found his old form and was ready for Game 4 of the American League Championship Series, when the Indians had to beat the Mariners.

me. If we wait until tomorrow, we can lose that game, too. Then we're done."

That night, Dennis Martinez won the first post-season game of his 20-year career. He won one of the biggest games in the history of the Indians franchise.

I sat there in the Kingdome, mesmerized by Martinez and by the Indians.

I never thought I'd see this. I never thought I'd see the Indians in the World Series. Even in 1995. Even when their record made them The Best Team In Baseball. Somehow, I feared that the best wouldn't be good enough. Something would happen to the Indians. Something always had.

The Indians last won a pennant in 1954. I was born in 1955.

I had heard about Cleveland teams like this. I had heard about Lou Boudreau and 1948. I had heard about 1954 and the team that had won more games than any American League team before or since. But those were like family folk tales, passed down from one generation to the next. They grew more mysterious and distant with each passing year until they became stories of When The Dinosaurs Roamed The Earth. I knew these stories were true; I just never thought I'd see the events happen again.

Then came 1994 and the new ballpark. Then came the 1995 season and the Indians who seemed to never lose. Then came Game 6 and the American League pennant as Dennis Martinez beat Seattle, 4-0.

I could see it. I knew it was real. But, somehow, I couldn't believe it. That was how it felt.

I knew exactly what Mike Hargrove meant when, after the game, he said: "I still have this feeling of disbelief — like it is happening, but it can't be happening. I still am pinching myself to make sure that this is what is happening to Mike Hargrove and the Cleveland Indians."

Hargrove had invested 14 years of his life in this quest, starting when he joined the Tribe as a player in 1979 and continuing as he managed at every level of the farm system. He had taken over a team that lost 105 games in 1991. He had said he always wanted to be here when the Indians finally won, but he had to wonder when that would happen . . . if it would happen . . . and if he'd still be alive to see it.

To fully appreciate what the Indians did on Oct. 17, 1995, you had to be in the Kingdome. You had to hear 58,489 fans shake the building and cheer against the Indians on every pitch, trying to carry the Mariners home on a wave of raw emotion.

Hill fired seven scoreless innings as the Tribe rolled, 7-0.

"What Kenny did against Seattle made the trade worthwhile — that one game alone," O'Dowd said. "He threw great, but, understand, he wasn't throwing anything like that when we traded for him. It was the work we did with the coaching staff that really paid off."

Hill's performance restored the Tribe's confidence. Then with Hershiser on the mound, they won again in Game 5, 3-2. They flew all night to Seattle, one victory away from their first pennant in 41 years.

Three hours before he was to pitch the most important game in the last 41 years of Cleveland Indians history, Dennis Martinez sat in the lobby of the Crown Center Hotel in Seattle.

Beacon Journal baseball writer Sheldon Ocker and I were surprised to see him sitting alone as we entered the lobby.

"Hey, what are you guys doing?" Dennis asked us.

We had come in from lunch. Martinez said he was waiting for a friend.

Martinez was wired. He loves to talk anyway, and the importance of the game had him in search of an audience.

That was us.

Martinez said that his shoulder was sore, his elbow ached and his knee just wouldn't do what it was told.

"Right now, I'm a waste physically," he said.

Ocker and I had heard this before — often. Dennis Martinez loves to discuss his ailments. The first time people hear the tale of woe they are convinced that he should be rushed to the nearest hospital, that he is a 40-year-old man knocking on death's door.

But Ocker and I had known Martinez for years. This was no reason for alarm; this was just was Dennis being Dennis. And we knew there was some truth to his story at the end of the season he would need knee surgery.

"And because my knee hurt, it caused my elbow to hurt," Martinez said, launching into his own rendition of "My knee bone is connected to the elbow bone . . . and the elbow bone is connected to the shoulder bone and . . . "

"A mess," he repeated. "That is what I am."

We laughed.

Then he laughed. "I *am*," he said, smiling.

Martinez talked about the first five games of the championship series, about how if the Indians had played well, there would have been no need for a Game 6. He critiqued the strategies employed by both teams; he liked some of the moves and disagreed with others.

Ocker saw several people heading into a conference room in the corner of the lobby. "Hey, Dennis, you ought to go talk to that meeting," he said.

"What meeting?" Martinez asked. "I'll go. I always talk to meetings."

Martinez thought the meeting might be one for members of Alcoholics Anonymous. At such meetings he regularly gives testimony about his own battle with booze and his salvation through the AA program.

"Dennis, I think it's some kind of computer meeting," I said. "But they probably would rather listen to you anyway."

"I bet you are right," he said. "I give good talks."

Any conversation with Dennis Martinez is liable to wind up in an unexpected direction. He once launched into a discussion of lawn care — right out of the blue. "I cut it myself," he said. "I do it because I like it, not because I'm too cheap to hire a guy to do it."

There is a reason that Martinez is known as "El Presidente," and it's not just because a fledgling political party in Nicaragua wants him to run for office when he retires from baseball. He has a gift for gab, and he talks like he pitches — working every angle. And that Tuesday in Seattle, he was trying to make Ocker and me believe that he had no chance against Randy Johnson in the Kingdome.

"Guys like Orel (Hershiser) and Randy Johnson — I'm not in their class," he said.

Ocker and I didn't buy it. And neither did Martinez. After all, he had won 231 games and was on the 1995 All-Star team.

But we knew why he was worried. He was the losing pitcher in Game 1, when Mariners rookie Bob Wolcott beat the Tribe, 3-2, in the Kingdome. Martinez again would be pitching in the Kingdome in front of more than 58,000 screaming converts who had just discovered the religion of baseball in the previous month. He was matched against Randy Johnson, who had seemed never to lose in 1995.

On his bad days, Martinez would complain that *he* was always the one who had to face the other team's best pitcher. "It's always *me,*" he would say. "No wonder they call me 'Mr. No Decision.' "

But in reality Martinez would have it no other way. He had been the ace of the Indians pitching staff since signing with the Tribe before the 1994 season, and his record was 23-11 with the Cleveland team. He wanted the ball in Game 6.

"It would be nice to win the game that puts Cleveland in the World Series," he finally admitted. "It would be something they can remember me doing."

He tried to paint a smiling face on the day and said he was glad the game would be in a dome.

"I've never worn long sleeves when I pitch," he said. "It doesn't feel right."

Once, when Martinez was a young pitcher with the Orioles, he beat the Indians on a frigid, windy, Godforsaken night at the old Cleveland Stadium. When the game was over, he shook his head and said, "When it gets this cold in Nicaragua, people die!"

Martinez had been scheduled to pitch Game 5 against the Mariners at Jacobs Field. But the temperature was headed down into the 40s and 30s, and Martinez's shoulder refused to obey his command to loosen up. Mike Hargrove was wise enough to switch Orel Hershiser to that game and to give Martinez the Kingdome, where Dennis could pitch in short sleeves.

"I supported Mike's decision all the way," Martinez said. "Orel was the right man for the job Sunday."

As we listened to Martinez, I thought about how he had been a big-leaguer longer than the Seattle franchise had been in existence. Martinez had pulled on a Baltimore uniform late in the 1976 season; the Mariners began playing in 1977 and finally made it to the playoffs in 1995.

The last time Martinez's team had made a post-season appearance was 1983.

Then, he had hit the bottom of the bottle and gone from one of the Orioles' top starters to the last man in their bullpen. "I didn't pitch in th playoffs or the World Series," he said. "I was fine physically, but a was mentally."

The only things he looked forward to were the post-game cele tions, where the booze flowed. He was 28 years old and trying to kill self by age 30.

"I've learned a lot over the years," he said. "I know that it i important how you are mentally than physically. I was a stronger, ier pitcher back then, but I'm a better pitcher now because I'm

Then he began to worry again about Game 6.

"I just hope these guys don't think, 'Well, if we don't get th we've got Game 7,' " he said. "The pitcher can only do so m want to feel like I'm alone out there. I can't win this ga Those guys have got to have their heads in the game; they

To be in Seattle on that night was to know why Manager Mike Hargrove called the Kingdome "The Mouth of the Lion."

I sat there in the teeth of that lion, and I watched Dennis Martinez do something even Bob Feller couldn't do. He won a game in the post-season, and he did it against a pitcher who was like Feller in his prime. When he took the mound, Martinez was convinced that no one gave him a chance against Randy Johnson, a man who hadn't lost a game since Aug. 1.

Martinez was like many Indians fans. He had a feeling that time was running out. So he went out and pitched the game of his life. In the words of Seattle Manager Lou Piniella, "Dennis went inside and outside with his pitches. He changed speeds. He threw to spots. He was like a surgeon out there."

He cut the heart out of Randy Johnson and the Seattle Mariners.

Knowing that he had to be as perfect as any 40-year-old pitcher could be, he went to Hargrove before the game. He asked for his personal catcher, 38-year-old Tony Pena, rather than Sandy Alomar, who usually starts. Some managers would have said, "Hey, no one makes out the lineup but me." Some would have argued with Martinez. But Hargrove looked into those piercing brown eyes and at the leathery face that has seen so much pain and come back from the depths of alcoholism.

Hargrove knew that Martinez was going to war and wanted Pena in the foxhole. Hargrove knew that a manager must know more than strategy. He knew that how the players felt before a game was a key to winning. So Hargrove wrote Pena's name in the lineup.

"When Dennis asked for me, it made my heart feel so good," Pena said. "We were in this together."

Orel Hershiser often talked about "the sense of urgency surrounding this team because of its history."

That is what Martinez and Pena brought to Game 6 in Seattle.

"Dennis was so intense, he didn't hear the noise," Pena said. "It was like we were the hand and the glove, working together. If we had to win that game 1-0, we could have done it."

Instead, Martinez left after seven scoreless innings. He left with his team owning a 4-0 lead when 22-year-old Julian Tavarez took over in the bottom of the eighth. Tavarez kept the Mariners down for an inning, and then for the ninth Hargrove handed the ball to Jose Mesa, who threw another zero on the scoreboard to put his exclamation mark on Tribe history.

Hargrove managed like he had all season: He made his plan and stuck to it. But that makes this game sound too cold, too clinical.

As Dennis Martinez beat the Mariners, I thought about how he was born in 1955, the year after the Indians' last pennant, and how this pitcher had won 231 big-league games but none in the post-season.

There was one other thing that had happened when Sheldon Ocker and I were with Martinez in the hotel lobby before the game. Bob Feller stopped by. Feller is the greatest pitcher in the history of the Cleveland franchise. His one disappointment in baseball is never having won a post-season game. Martinez faced those same demons in Game 6; he had the history of the franchise and of his own post-season failures on his shoulders. Feller wished Martinez luck, and Dennis said he'd take all the luck he could get.

But Dennis Martinez didn't need any. Neither did the Indians. Great ones never do.

18

NOT-SO-FOND MEMORIES

For those who can recall the last time the Indians won a pennant, the Tribe's uprising in 1995 led to some scary flashbacks. Remember 1954, they said.

But most Indians fans weren't around for 1954. They had only heard about the team that won 111 games — still an American League record. They had only heard about Bob Lemon, Early Wynn, Mike Garcia, Bob Feller and all the others who made up what may have been the greatest pitching staff ever.

But the 1954 Indians — supposedly a team for the ages — were swept by the New York Giants in the World Series.

How could a team have a 111-43 record in the regular season and then not even win *one* World Series game? And if it happened in 1954, could it haunt the 1995 Indians with their sparkling 100-44 record?

Before the Indians opened the playoffs against Boston, I had talked with Al Rosen, the third baseman and captain of that 1954 team. He was 71, retired, and living in Rancho Mirage, Calif. He was also keeping tabs on the Tribe.

"They're unbeatable," he said. "Look at how they played after they clinched. They just kept winning. It is like they are zeroed-in on a championship. I expect them to go all the way. The only team that I can see giving them trouble is Atlanta because the Braves have great pitching."

Rosen called it typical Tribe luck to win more games than any other team in baseball, yet still have to work their way through a new three-tiered playoff system in which they didn't even have the home-field advantage.

"But I just don't think it will matter much to these guys," Rosen said. "Young teams have a certain exuberance about them. They don't buckle to pressure, and they have enough veterans to help them in the clubhouse. I've always thought that Dennis Martinez is a terrific big-game pitcher, and I expect Orel Hershiser to rise to the occasion. He loves the spotlight."

Rosen was a general manager for 20 years, running the New York Yankees, the Houston Astros and the San Francisco Giants before retiring in 1992. He was astounded by the Tribe's lineup.

"In 1954, we had awesome pitching, but we couldn't hit like these guys," he said. "Their seventh hitter (Paul Sorrento) has 25 homers. The centerfielder (Kenny Lofton) is a special player, and the second baseman (Carlos Baerga) is a double-special player. I love having Eddie Murray on my team at a time like this."

Rosen left the best for last — Albert Belle.

"Just who is going to get him out?" he asked. "I've seen his last three homers on TV. I've seen the Indians play a lot on TV this year, and let me tell you something about Albert Belle's home runs — they don't just clear the fence."

And Rosen had even more to say about Belle.

"He has tremendous command of home plate," he said. "Pitch him inside and he pulls the ball out to left field. Pitch him away, and he hits it out to right-center. He is so strong, so focused. He studies the pitchers so well. I mean, how many times has he been fooled and looked bad swinging at a pitch lately?"

Until Belle hit 50 homers this year, Rosen had the Tribe record with 43 back in 1953.

"I'm not surprised Albert broke my record," he said. "Heck, they broke Lou Gehrig's record (for playing in consecutive major league games), and that was one that I never thought would be broken. I'm kind of surprised it lasted this long. There was one year when I really thought Rocky Colavito (with 42 homers in 1959) might do it. Albert Belle is going to break a lot of records before he is through."

What about Roger Maris' record of hitting 61 homers in 1961?

"Suppose Albert started a year like he finished this one," Rosen said. "Suppose he got this kind of momentum going early in the season. Yes, I can see him doing it. He's a big, strong guy who is a smart hitter playing in a hitter-friendly park and surrounded by a lot of other good hitters. If everything went right, Albert could do it."

And the Indians?

"When you're not playing in these games, a part of you believes that no one should beat your team in a series like this," Rosen said. "The other part has you so fearful that you will lose, even though you have the better team.

"But I just don't think it will happen — not to the Indians. They are the best team I've seen all year, and one of the best Indians teams ever, so don't worry about them."

As I listened to Rosen, I wondered what had happened in 1954. That team was a collection of talented but high-strung individuals, men whose fire was shrewdly cooled by outwardly tranquil manager Al Lopez.

There was Larry Doby, who led the league with 32 homers and 126 RBI in 1954.

"Larry could do everything," Rosen recalled. "He should have been the best player in the American League. But he was a victim of the black-white thing that was really bad in our country at the time. He couldn't believe that when he got to the big leagues, he was 'a dirty nigger,' and he was called that. Those things ate him up."

The Indians second baseman was Bobby Avila, the 1954 batting champion with a .341 average. He also was one of the first big-league Mexican players in baseball history.

"He looked like Cesar Romero, and I know that he was our only Latin player," Rosen said. "He could be sullen and a little moody. In retrospect, he probably was under more pressure than most of us realized."

Indeed he was. Avila had stomach ulcers and was under doctor's orders to drink a half-gallon of milk every day during the 1954 season.

"A really interesting guy was Early Wynn," Rosen said. "He had some Indian blood in him. If he were coming down a mountain after me, I'd shoot myself before he got to me. Early could be mean, miserable, cantankerous, obstinate — and I consider him one of my best friends."

Then Rosen laughed at his memories of Wynn, who won 23 games in 1954.

"In the spring of 1954, we played a spring-training game, and Wally Westlake was in left field," Rosen said. "Wynn was pitching and a ball was hit into the gap, and Westlake didn't go after it full-tilt. That night we were in a restaurant and Wynn came up to Westlake. The whole team was there. Wynn said, 'Listen, you no-good SOB. If you ever short-leg a ball on me again, I'll tear your head off.' No one said a word because everyone knew that Early was serious."

The Tribe's other 23-game winner was Bob Lemon.

"One of my best friends in the world," Rosen said. "He ought to will his liver to the Smithsonian Institute. Everyone knew that Lemon drank, but he never drank the day before or the day he pitched. In a lot of ways, he was like Al Lopez — very steady and reliable. I hired him to manage when I was general manager of the Yankees because he was so steady."

Bob Feller's nickname was "Incy," because "he was the first ballplayer any of us knew who incorporated himself like a business," Rosen said. "He had a massive ego, but there wasn't a bad bone in his body. And he was in great condition."

In fact, it was Feller who led the sprints and exercises to keep Wynn and Mike Garcia in reasonable shape, as both right-handers had weight problems.

"I loved Mike Garcia because he was so gentle off the field," Rosen said. "Until he was 15 years old, he rode horses and wanted to be a jockey. Then he grew into the guy we called 'The Big Bear.' "

Garcia won 19 games in 1954.

"They always talked about how Early Wynn would get mad and throw at hitters," Rosen said. "But Garcia knocked down more hitters than Early. He could be fierce and frightening."

Rosen is Jewish, and 1954 was a time when there were few Jews in baseball.

"It wasn't that big of a problem for me," he said. "The guy who paved the way was Hank Greenberg, who played in the 1930s. He was the Jewish Jackie Robinson because of all the abuse he took."

In 1950, it was Greenberg, by then the Tribe general manager, who made the decision to replace the popular Ken Keltner at third base with Rosen.

"The fans got on me for bringing up a Jew to replace a nice Catholic boy, but it was the right thing to do," Greenberg wrote in his autobiography, *In My Time*.

Many of the Indians of 1954 were solid, quiet, dependable guys, according to Rosen. He mentioned shortstop George Strickland; first baseman Vic Wertz; outfielder Al Smith, "the consummate pro," and catcher Jim Hegan, "the backbone of the team."

"He (Hegan) roomed with Bob Lemon, yet he never drank," Rosen said. "He had the looks of a movie star and was like Baryshnikov behind the plate. He had a wonderful voice and loved to sing and dance. He was the kind of person you just wanted to be in the same room with."

Two words: Dusty Rhodes. They sum up what hit the Indians in the 1954 World Series.

Until the 1954 Series, not many baseball fans outside of New York had ever heard of Dusty Rhodes. Afterward, most forgot him. But for four days, Tribe fans learned to curse the name of James Lamar Rhodes.

Rhodes began doing his damage in Game 1, when his three-run pinch homer in the 10th inning gave the New York Giants a 5-2 victory.

"It had all the harsh, crushing quality of a poached egg," Franklin Lewis wrote in the old Cleveland Press. "It was a pop fly that shot almost straight up toward the second baseman and was borne by a friendly wind to the wall, some 260 feet away. Only in the Polo Grounds could it have been such."

In Game 2, Rhodes hit another homer off Early Wynn and also drove in a run with a base hit; the Giants won 3-1. In Game 3, he drove in two more runs with a pinch hit. For the series, he was 4-for-6 with two homers and seven RBI. Compare that to the entire Indians team, which had only nine RBI.

Rhodes played for seven years and was a career .253 hitter with 54 homers. His defense was shaky, and he was best known as a pinch hitter. But in 1954, he batted .341 with 15 homers in 164 at-bats.

"Really, the guy just caught lightning in a bottle," Rosen recalled. "The 1954 World Series was Dusty Rhodes' time on Earth."

Forty-some years later, Al Lopez still didn't know what had happened to his Cleveland Indians in the 1954 World Series.

"Being swept in four games? We had four Hall of Famers on that pitching staff," he said. "The only thing I can say is that we had a slump at the absolute worst time."

Lopez was 87 in the fall of 1995, the oldest surviving member of the Hall of Fame. He lived in a ranch home that he bought in 1959 on Tampa Bay in Florida. He talked about his Big Four of Lemon, Feller, Wynn and Garcia (the only one of the four who didn't make the Hall of Fame), and about how another Hall of Famer — Hal Newhouser — was in the bullpen.

"What pitching we had," said Lopez of the team that had a 2.78 earned-run average, the American League's best in 1954.

Lopez's players used to say that the only way they could tell when their usually placid manager was worried was when the veins on his forehead rose just a bit. Well, four decades after the 1954 World Series, the mention of those games makes his brow furrow and the veins rise.

"I have no answers," he said with the same face he wore after any tough defeat.

Bob Lemon once said that the worst thing about losing "was walking in the dressing room and seeing Al just sitting there, staring at his toes.

He never said a word — just looked at those toes for hours."

When the Indians fell behind the Giants 3-0 in the Series, Lopez was told that no team had ever come from a 3-0 deficit to win a seven-game series.

"No team ever won 111 games before, like my team," he said.

But the Indians lost Game 4, 7-4. Lopez was left with nothing to do but stare at his feet.

Lopez was known as "El Senor," and he was a calming presence in the dugout.

"He gets in no bitter arguments, utters no fiery quotes and never chews out a player in front of others," Sports Illustrated wrote. "The players take his cue and do their job with a minimum of fuss."

Lopez made it look easy. He managed the Indians for six years, winning one pennant and finishing second five other times.

"He was understanding, compassionate and the kind of guy you want next to you in a barroom brawl," Rosen recalled. "We called him the 'Silent Senor.' I heard him dress down a couple of guys in his office once — he fired them. But there was never anything phony about him. You know, after the 1954 World Series, Al started to think that not much else good was going to happen to him in Cleveland. It's hard to imagine the impact today. But to all of us who were there, it's still an unbelievable thing — what happened to the Indians in that World Series."

As for Al Rosen, all he wanted to do was sleep off that 1954 World Series.

"My in-laws were in town for the games," he said. "We had a baby boy at the time. I called them from the clubhouse after the fourth game and asked if they could stay and baby-sit for another day . . . I mean, we had a chance to be among the 10 greatest teams of all time, then . . . " His voice trailed off.

"For a team to win 111 games and lose the way we did with our great pitching — it was a very helpless feeling. The dressing room was like being at the wake of your best friend. A few guys cried, but a lot of us were just emotionally spent."

When the Indians lost that final game of 1954 at home, the New York Times' Arthur Daley wrote: "A breathless hush fell over the sprawling Stadium. It was so quiet you could almost hear a heart break. No one spoke a kind word about the deceased. The Indians died friendless and alone."

Rosen knew the feeling.

"After we lost that fourth game, my wife and I checked into the old Statler Hotel," he said. "I bought a bottle of Scotch and some sleeping pills. I was a guy who hated to take anything, even an aspirin. Anyway, I had a couple of drinks, took two sleeping pills and told my wife that I was going to rest for awhile. I slept for 36 straight hours."

When Rosen awoke, he discovered that the Sporting News had called the 1954 Indians "the most overrated team in World Series history" and said that the only reason they won a record 111 games was "because the American League must have been a bunch of pushovers."

The New York Times said: "The Indians played dull, spiritless, maladroit baseball . . . it was a disgrace."

Rosen said you had to be in the Indians' spikes to fully understand.

"Year after year, we were in second place to the Yankees," he said. "After awhile, you get so sick of being a bridesmaid. Even in 1954, everyone was waiting for us to fold and blow the pennant to the Yankees."

Lopez had been hired to manage the Indians in 1951, and he led the team to three consecutive second-place finishes — all to New York. On Sept. 12, 1954, when the Yankees came to Cleveland for a double-header, they kept screaming "chokers" at the Indians. But on that damp, rainy day, 84,587 fans packed the Stadium and saw Lemon and Wynn shut down the Yankees. When the afternoon was over, the Indians had an 8½-game-lead, and the pennant race was over.

"For us, *that* was winning the World Series," Rosen said. "We didn't care about the 111 games (which topped the American League record of 110 victories by the 1927 Yankees). We didn't care about anything but beating New York."

When the Indians did clinch the pennant, more than 250,000 fans jammed downtown Cleveland as the players rolled down Euclid Avenue in convertibles.

Rosen had been the American League's most valuable player in 1953, hitting .336 with 43 homers and 145 RBI as a third baseman. But he agreed to play first base in 1954 so rookie Rudy Regalado would have a chance to break in at third.

"Can you imagine an MVP doing that today?" Rosen asked. "But Al Lopez asked me to do that, and if Al wanted me to run through a wall, I ran through a wall."

Regalado lasted only six weeks because he was staying up late on the nightclub circuit "and would come to the ballpark practically drunk from lack of sleep," wrote Tribe general manager Hank Greenberg in his autobiography.

Rosen was switched back to third base. In a sense, it was too late. He had fractured his right index finger while trying to catch a ground ball at first, and he spent much of 1954 swinging with one hand on the bat. Even so, he still hit .300 with 24 homers and 102 RBI. He also broke his nose. That was no big deal. Rosen said he broke his nose 13 times during his career.

"The really bad thing was, by the World Series, I had a terrible hamstring pull and could barely run," he said. "Larry Doby was in the same shape. He couldn't even tape his leg because it was so raw and bleeding from the taping all year. They took part of an inner tube, wrapped that around his leg and taped over it."

Doby, the Indians centerfielder, also was hindered by a shoulder badly bruised from sliding into second base during the final week of the season.

"Back then, you just didn't sit out many games like today," Rosen said. "The schedule said 154 games and you wanted to play 154 games."

Managers also liked to use their best players every day. So the Tribe literally limped into the World Series and hit bottom in Game 4 when Lemon tried to pitch on only two days' rest.

"You can talk about how we didn't get a break, and we didn't in the first two games," Rosen said. "But in the end, I just think our tank was empty. We had nothing left. It was as if that team was not destined to reach its true destiny."

For that reason, Rosen was pulling hard for the Tribe in 1995.

"They have a great team, too, and they were healthier than we were heading into the playoffs," he said. "I love this team, and I just don't expect them to be a repeat of what happened in 1954."

19

TALES FOR TOMORROW

When the World Series began, I had a hard time concentrating on the Atlanta Braves. I knew the Braves had a great pitching staff. I knew this was their third trip to the World Series in the last five years. I knew they were what stood between the Indians and Cleveland's first world title since 1948. But I just couldn't get all that excited about Atlanta.

To me, the World Series was about something far more personal than a match with some team from the National League. The World Series was about my father.

I know that it's a cliche to say that baseball is fathers and sons. I know that some kids don't have fathers. I know that sometimes it's mothers and sons — or daughters. Heck, Tony Pena's mom is the one who taught him how to play. "My father didn't even know on which hand he should put the glove," Pena told me.

But it was my father, Tom Pluto, who gave me the Indians. He held my hand and took me to the games at the old Cleveland Stadium throughout the 1960s and early 1970s. He bought me those flat Cokes and the stale popcorn that was sold at the concession stands — food we always thought was left over from the Browns season. As I grew older and sports became my business, when I needed to remind myself of what the games were really about, I thought of my father.

I would have loved for him to be at the playoffs and the World Series. He was entitled to that, but life doesn't always give us what we deserve.

As I've mentioned before, my father is retired. He lives in Sarasota, Fla., where he continues to battle a major stroke that he suffered in September of 1993. He is 75 years old and in reasonably decent health, given what the stroke has done to his brain. But he cannot travel far and isn't very comfortable anywhere but in his own house.

You want to know why the Indians making the 1995 World Series was so important to me? Simply because then my father could watch the games on TV.

My father can't move his right arm and can barely move his right leg. A stroke is like a blowout in a computer's memory. Certain signals get crossed and stay crossed. In addition to becoming paralyzed on his right side, my father lost his ability to speak. For the most part, he can now say one word: man.

How he says "man" tells you how he feels.

Sometimes he can say that one word — man — and it will bring tears to your eyes. That is what happened during the Indians' run through the American League playoffs.

Major league baseball cut this ridiculous deal with something called the Baseball Network, which decided that not all the playoff games needed to be televised nationally.

My father knew that the Indians were in the post-season because ESPN told him so. He watches ESPN constantly during the day, even the volleyball games and tractor pulls. ESPN would tell him that the Indians were playing Seattle that night, and he would wait for the games. He knew that playoff games were televised. He would take the TV remote, search for the Indians and only find the Atlanta Braves and the National League playoffs.

"Man. . . *man* . . . *MAN*!" he would yell.

More channel surfing. More Braves games.

No Indians.

"Oh, man." And his voice would drop to a whisper.

He became so discouraged one night that he ended up watching bowling instead of the National League playoffs.

That is why I hated the Baseball Network.

There are millions of people all over the country who are shut-ins, stuck in rest homes. Their days often are spent waiting for a ballgame at night. You can say it shouldn't be that way. You can say that the people like my father could read a book instead of watching the games. Well, I have news for you. One of the terrible things the stroke did to my father was shatter the part of the brain that enables him to read. He does a pretty good job of deciphering nouns, but verbs and any sort of complicated sentence confuse him.

I sent him copies of the Beacon Journal's special sports sections on the playoffs, because they featured huge color pictures of the Indians. He would spread them out on the sofa, right next to his favorite chair. He would stare at pictures of the different players and at the stories with my picture and name on them. He would show them to people who came to visit.

Who knows what he was thinking? Maybe he was asking, "Why are the Indians in the paper, but not on TV?"

Watching sports on TV is as good as it gets for people such as my father. When he was told that the Indians wouldn't be on — that the people running baseball decided that people living in the South only would be interested in the playoff games between the Atlanta Braves and the Cincinnati Reds — well, he just couldn't believe it.

You could have an M.B.A. from Harvard and not understand the thinking behind the Baseball Network. So how was I supposed to explain this to my father?

My father is a lifetime Indians fan. He was born in 1920, the year the team won its first World Series. When the Indians were an embarrassment in the 1960s and 1970s, he was a paying customer. He cared when it wasn't easy to say you were an Indians fan.

All over the South there were retired folks from northern Ohio whose lives would have been made better if they could have watched the Tribe in the playoffs. But they couldn't, and there was no excuse for that.

In the end, there was only one thing I could tell my father: "Dad, the bums that run baseball really don't care about you."

But, thankfully, the Indians beat Seattle and were able to play the National League champion Atlanta Braves — at least the World Series was still televised nationally.

Just the thought of seeing those games made my father nearly as happy as the day when he first came home from the rest home after nine months of post-stroke therapy. The Indians were in the World Series, and he was still alive to see it. He would be able to watch the games from his favorite chair.

I talked about my father to Tribe coach Buddy Bell. The Indians in the World Series made us think of someone special.

Bell's 66-year-old father, Gus, had died suddenly on May 7, 1995 from a heart attack.

"I wish he was at the games with my family," said Bell, who had seven of his relatives at the games. "But I could be a dogcatcher, and I couldn't imagine missing my dad any more than I do right now."

Bell said his father's death "was a bolt out of the blue." He hadn't had any signs of heart trouble.

"On the day he died, he was supposed to drive up from Cincinnati to Cleveland to see our game," Bell said. "David (Buddy's son and Gus' grandson) had just been promoted from (Class AAA) Buffalo and he wanted to watch us all in the big leagues together."

The Bells are one of baseball's premier families. Gus played for 15 years, mostly as a power-hitting outfielder with the Cincinnati Reds. Buddy was an 18-year big-leaguer, primarily with the Tribe and the Texas Rangers. David was a 22-year-old infielder when the Indians brought him to Cleveland in May.

During the 1994 baseball strike, Gus and Buddy went to see David play for the Tribe's Class AAA Charlotte team. They sat in the Bob Uecker seats, away from everyone else, so they wouldn't be recognized by fans and take any attention away from David and his team.

"My dad never made that much money in baseball because the salaries weren't anything like today, or even when I played," Bell said. "After he retired from baseball, he worked his butt off. He sold cars. He sold real estate. He tried scouting, but didn't like it because all the travel took him away from his family. Then he and my mother opened an embroidery business, and that worked out pretty well for them. But my dad didn't see me play much when I was in high school because he was always working. I understood, but I'd be at my games and I'd sort of look out of the corner of my eye to see if he was there. When I did see him, it really made me feel good. The funny thing is that my father has seen my sons play more than I have because I have been away so much with baseball and he was at home and had slowed down (his work schedule)."

As I listened to Bell, I thought of my father and of how he'd slip away from his job at the old Fisher-Fazio food warehouse to watch me play baseball at Benedictine High. First we went to Indians games together when I was a kid, and then he went to see me play.

"Everyone thinks that we'd sit around the dinner table and talk baseball all night," Bell said. "But we hardly did at all. My father never pressured me to play, just as I never pressured my sons."

Bell paused for a moment.

"For his funeral, all of my brothers and sisters wrote him letters," he said. "We had a friend read them at the eulogy. I wrote about how my father was my best friend and how he was very wise, but he never took himself too seriously. He knew when to hug you and when to kick you in the butt."

Buddy Bell was 43 when he told me this. He said that he used to call his father every two or three days. He missed his dad, missed hearing his voice. He said how much he would have loved to talk to his dad about the World Series.

As I listened to Bell, I was grateful that my father was still alive to see these games. After the season, I would visit my father in Florida, and the World Series would give us something very good to talk about, something to help take his mind off what time and fate have done to his brain and his body.

The Indians opened their first World Series in 41 years in Atlanta, and it seemed like they were asleep.

Greg Maddux, who started for the Braves, is probably the best pitcher this decade has seen. His fastball is only slightly above average, but his pitches sink and continually populate the black edges of home plate. Everything is on the inside corner or the outside corner. If he does miss the inside corner, the ball rides right up into the hitter's hands, often sawing the bat right off as the batter tries to hit that inside pitch. If the outside pitches aren't on the corner, they slide a few inches off home plate. Nothing he throws is down the middle, and most of it is knee high.

The Indians managed just two hits off him. If it hadn't been for some shoddy Atlanta fielding and Kenny Lofton's legs, the Tribe would not even have scored. Instead, they lost the opener, 3-2.

The next night Dennis Martinez started for Cleveland. He wasn't sharp and allowed four runs in less than six innings. Tom Glavine pitched for the Braves, and the Indians really didn't hit him that well, either. Atlanta won again, 4-3.

The Tribe headed home having lost the first two games of the Series. The Indians also had used their top two pitchers — Orel Hershiser and Martinez. Whispers of the sweep of 1954 returned — especially since Manager Mike Hargrove had Charles Nagy scheduled to start Game 3.

Nagy does not come across as a happy man. You get the feeling that if he ever really smiled — one of those ear-to-ear grins — his jaw might break. He goes through life like a man who's always worried about having enough insurance because he is *convinced* that something terrible is about to happen.

That is why Manager Mike Hargrove and pitching coach Mark Wiley spent so much time telling Nagy that he was indeed a good pitcher.

They would tell Nagy: "Trust yourself, you have won a lot of games in this league . . . trust your stuff, you have a better arm than you think you do."

Hargrove knew that if Nagy lost Game 3, it would be over — no team had ever been down 0-3 and come back to win the World Series. If the

Indians lost, they would be staring at a sweep and feeling as depressed as Nagy usually looks.

Publicly, Hargrove talked about how Nagy had been one of the delights of the Indians' post-season. Who beat Boston in Fenway Park to wrap up the first round of the playoffs? None other than this taciturn right-hander from Fairfield, Conn. Who matched Randy Johnson pitch for pitch in Game 3 of the American League Championship Series? It was Nagy, who held Seattle to one run in eight innings. Who finished the regular season by winning five of his last six starts? OK, you get the idea.

"I think Charlie has been overlooked," Hargrove said. "Not by the people in baseball, but by the media. Charlie is a very quiet person, who goes about his business very well. He's very unassuming and doesn't beat his own drum."

When you talk to Nagy, you almost want to yell for a medic to check his pulse. He is so soft-spoken, so deadpan, that you wonder what he's hiding.

"Charlie would make a great card player because he'd never tip his hand," said Tribe General Manager John Hart. "He keeps things to himself very well."

Nagy won 16 games for the Tribe, but he did it with a 4.55 earned-run average. Some insist that an asterisk should have been put next to his victory total because he was carried by the Tribe's big bats. He had a streak of eight starts in which he was 6-0 with a 4.00 ERA, but in those games the Indians averaged eight runs every time he took the mound.

He grew up in New England, where words are not to be wasted and most men look at the world through a cracked mirror, knowing it is a cold, hard place. The Indians drafted him out of the University of Connecticut in 1988. He was a member of the 1988 Olympic team, and he made it to the major leagues by 1990. In 1992, at the age of 25, he was the ace of the Indians staff, winning 17 games. Then Nagy blew out his shoulder. He gritted his teeth and pitched through excruciating pain for two months before submitting to reconstructive surgery in 1993.

"After an operation like that, it just takes a while for a player to get all his arm strength back," Wiley said. "He won 10 games for us last year (1994), but by the end of season, his arm was pretty tired. He probably would have had to miss a turn or two if the strike hadn't come."

In the spring of 1995, the 6-foot-3, 200-pounder reported to camp weighing much closer to 190. His wife is a marathoner, and he had been training with her. Nagy's way of coping with stress is to run or sweat on the Stairmaster. During the strike he was the Indians' player representative, and he found the pressure of the situation to be an enormous burden.

Nagy started the season slowly, and there were times when his shoulder just didn't feel right and he lost confidence in his ability to pitch inside. Then he became Nagy The Nibbler, even though his fastball was an above-average 90 mph — quite capable of serving as a power saw to cut bats right out of the hands of hitters.

Wiley and Hargrove often had to remind Nagy of that. They would say: You throw harder than you think. You need to pitch inside and you have the arm to do it. If you are timid and keep throwing that fluff on the outside corner, the hitters are going to kill you.

In Game 3 of the World Series, Nagy pitched seven solid innings. At the end of that time, the Indians had a 5-3 lead over the Braves.

Then, for some strange reason, which sounded worse every time Hargrove tried to explain it, Hargrove allowed Nagy to open the eighth inning instead of going to the rested bullpen. By the time the top of the eighth inning was over, the Braves were ahead, 6-5.

Eventually the Indians won the game, 7-6, on an Eddie Murray RBI single in the 11th inning. The players rushed onto the field, mobbing Murray. In the dugout, Hargrove felt more a sense of relief than joy — he had dodged a bullet, and his team was still alive.

Before that Game 3 victory, Albert Belle embarrassed himself and the Indians when he cussed out NBC's Hannah Storm in the dugout.

To those who have been around Belle for years, this behavior was nothing new. He didn't just act this way around sportswriters and broadcasters. He didn't get nasty because he was under the World Series gun. Belle had been acting like a bully for years, and often he insulted fans for no reason other than the fact that he was "having a bad day."

Belle's treatment of Storm became an issue because the outburst occurred during the World Series, and he verbally attacked a person representing a TV network that was paying millions to broadcast the games.

NBC didn't even want to talk to Belle. The network had set up a camera and some lights in a corner of the dugout — something that was permitted before the game — and Storm was waiting to interview Kenny Lofton. Belle didn't like the TV crew being in his dugout, and he said so in the kind of language that would peel paint right off the walls. It was ugly and it was dumb — and Belle knew better.

As one Indians official often said, "Albert's people skills leave something to be desired."

A fellow who ran into Belle in the lobby of Seattle's Crown Center the previous week could attest to that. The man happened to walk close to Belle, who decided the fellow was infringing on his space. Belle didn't say: "Excuse me, would you mind moving?" No, Belle told the guy . . . actually, I won't print what Belle told the guy. Let's just say he put together a string of obscenities, insulting the man's sexuality among other things.

This gentleman told several Cleveland scribes: "That Albert Belle sure has a foul mouth."

Belle is the son of two teachers. He is from a middle-class home. He was an honors student in high school and did well at Louisiana State University. His twin brother Terry is an accountant in Memphis.

The point is that Belle didn't crawl out of some gutter — there are times when he just talks that way.

Obviously, he doesn't care. But just because you can hit home runs and make millions of dollars doesn't mean you have the right to resign from the human race when it suits you. It is true that a lot of other baseball stars have been slugs, far worse than Belle. Ty Cobb was a bigot who nearly beat a black man to death because of his race. Rogers Hornsby was a .400 hitter and one of the most surly SOBs ever to wear a uniform. Ted Williams could scowl and growl with the best of them.

But that doesn't make Belle's behavior right.

The day before Belle's explosion, I had talked to former Indian Andre Thornton. He never mentioned Belle's name, but his words were prophetic.

The closest Thornton ever came to a World Series was Game 3 in 1995, when he and his family were in the stands at Jacobs Field. He retired from baseball in 1987 after an 11-year career with the Tribe. He is one of the former Indians who deserves to walk across the national stage and have the likes of NBC's Bob Costas and Bob Uecker telling America his story. But Thornton was with the old Indians and his teams never finished higher than fifth place.

"In this lineup, I would have hit fifth or sixth," he said. "But when I played, I batted fourth. Most years there were very few power hitters around me. It would have been fun to play on a team like this."

Thornton is fourth on the Tribe's all-time home run list, and he led the team in home runs in seven different seasons. Now he is a successful businessman. He is known for his religious and charitable work.

"I wasn't like some guys who said that baseball was their life and all they had in life," he said. "But I also knew that it was a darn good job. I liked it. I was lucky to be able to play baseball all those years, and I wasn't afraid to let people get to know me through the media or by going out into the community."

Thornton lives in Chagrin Falls, Ohio, and he was one of the few Indians of his era (along with Rick Manning and Duane Kuiper) who lived year-round in northeast Ohio.

"I see some of these players who are about 25 years old and they are true stars — some of the best young players in the game — but they go and hide," Thornton said. "They don't want many people to know them. They figure that their job is to come to the park, play the game and leave. It doesn't have to be that way."

Thornton talked a little about his Indians, playing before 65,000 empty seats at the dismal old Cleveland Stadium, losing night after night.

"This is a special time in Cleveland baseball," Thornton said. "I see some of the Indians' players eating up the excitement, but a lot more of them should step forward and live it. They earned all the attention that is coming their way, so why hide from it? Why not enjoy it?"

Thornton said modern players are coming of age in a baseball world of deception and anger, and that is skewing their view of the game.

"It stems from all the labor-management problems," he said. "What do these young players see? Pettiness. They see people dodging the real issues. They hear name-calling. They see people running and hiding when things get tough, so that is what they learn to do. They make it such a business. It is disturbing when I hear a young player say, 'I'm going to play five years and then retire.' To me, that is like the guy saying he can't stand the game — that he is playing because he has to. You wonder what is eating at some of those guys. There are so many more unhappy players now, guys with a chip on their shoulder. I see too many young stars who have a poor relationship with the game and the people in baseball. That's sad because the things I treasure the most about my career are my relationships with the people I met through baseball."

Thornton was 46 in the fall of 1995. During his career, he was a man who never ran for cover. He answered to the fans and the media even after the bad days because he knew it was part of the job.

"You have to stand up to the scrutiny," he said. "Young players need to understand that people will write and say bad things about them when they play poorly, and they can't take it personally. If they accept the praise for playing well, then they have to take some of the criticism when they don't. They can't just say, 'I'm not talking to anybody.' They should realize that in 10 or 15 years, they'll look back and see that they played on a great team, and maybe they will wish they had enjoyed it more."

During the World Series, Albert Belle did nothing to help his national image — either on the field or off — but Kenny Lofton made folks stand up and cheer, and they weren't just Indians fans.

In the first inning of the first World Series game, Lofton's name was being mentioned in the same sentence with Babe Ruth's. It had been that kind of October for Kenny Lofton. OK, the subject was Babe Ruth's stolen bases, not his home runs. But Lofton's two steals in the first inning of Game 1 sent everyone to the record books and the search didn't end until they came to 1921, when Ruth stole two bases in the same inning of a World Series game.

Understand this about stealing bases: It hurts. Just ask Rickey Henderson, who has stolen more bases than anyone. Henderson says a base-stealer isn't like the Road Runner. He doesn't just go "beep-beep" and disappear in a cloud of dust.

"Your body takes a terrible beating," Henderson often said. "Your thighs and legs are bruised from all the sliding. Pitchers try to pick you off, and you have to dive back to first base. When you do steal, your legs and ankles are taking a pounding."

After awhile, the player simply gets tired of all the sprained ankles and pulled muscles. His heart (and maybe even his manager) says, "Go," but his head says, "Take a break." So the player steals when it means the most and has a direct impact on a close game — not just to pad his statistics.

That is why Henderson's three seasons of more than 100 steals are astounding. The last time he did it was in 1983, and he doubts it will ever happen again.

Lofton led the American League in stolen bases in each of the last four seasons. His best was 70 in 1993, and in 1995 he stole 54. To break 50, he ran wild in September, stealing 22.

But he also paid a price.

"We didn't want to advertise it, but Kenny was hurting in the Boston series," John Hart said. "He pulled his hamstring in the final regular-season game, and it was pretty tender. He just didn't trust his leg to even try to steal a base."

Lofton was frustrated and tentative in the three-game sweep of

Boston. He was only 2-for-13 at the plate. He had more strikeouts (three) and errors (two) than stolen bases (none). As usual, he was silent about his injury.

"Kenny has always played hurt for us, but he just doesn't like to talk about it," Hart said. "In his rookie year (1992), he played nearly half the season with a broken hamate bone in his left hand. This year he had a variety of injuries, and I really don't think we even saw the real Kenny Lofton until the final month of the regular season."

When Lofton is hurting, he becomes sullen and moody. In July of 1995, he pulled a muscle in his rib cage swinging at a pitch in batting practice. For a week he insisted it "wasn't that bad." But the muscle didn't heal, and the Indians had to put Lofton on the disabled list for the first time in his career. Even so, Lofton batted .310 for the season, with seven homers and 53 RBI, in addition to the 54 steals. And, yes, he was an All-Star for the second year in a row.

But 1995 wasn't a vintage Lofton year until the American League Championship Series and the World Series.

He was embarrassed by his statistics in the Boston series, and he cut loose against Seattle, determined to cement his image as the game's premier leadoff man in the minds of the media and the nation's baseball fans.

Lofton batted .467 against the Mariners and he had five stolen bases. He also took away at least three Mariner hits with dynamite catches in center field. His legs won at least two of those games.

Hargrove often talks about Lofton's legs "tilting the game in our direction," because his running puts so much pressure on the opponents.

The Atlanta Braves learned that, too.

"If there were two or three Kenny Loftons, facing Cleveland would be impossible," said Braves pitcher John Smoltz. "It's tough enough facing one Kenny Lofton — not just because he can run, but (because) he's a good hitter and so tough to keep off base."

In dealing with the media, Lofton finally broke out of his shell. He freely gave interviews and came across like a nice guy. That's the Lofton America saw on TV screens and in newspapers for most of October. Though he ended up hitting only .200 in the World Series, Lofton bought himself a lot of good will and respect with his excellent behavior and his electric base-running — he had six steals in the Series, more than the entire Atlanta team.

Lofton came to the realization that most members of the national media really were looking for reasons to sing his praises, and he learned that he could help them write the lyrics by talking with them for a few minutes.

It would take six games, but the Indians really lost the World Series in Game 4. The score was tied, 1-1, entering the seventh inning, when the Braves broke through against starter Ken Hill and the Tribe bullpen.

By the end of the game, it was so quiet you could hear the Indians' batting average drop. Tribe fans felt like wearing black instead of red and blue. Jacobs Field was no longer a ballpark; it was a church. This wasn't the World Series; it was a wake. The only thing missing was a few final words from the priest about how we had gathered together to pay last respects to a good friend.

Actually, nothing was needed to break the silence because the scoreboard screamed: Atlanta 5, Indians 2.

As the fans filed out of Jacobs Field, there were 43,578 bowed heads, their hoarse voices mere whispers. The streets were jammed, but the horns were quiet. You half-expected the cars to have little flags on their hoods and to be driven single-file to the cemetery. OK, it's not over until it's over, but this was as close to over as a World Series gets. Bad enough was being down, 3-1, in this seven-game series. Worse was having to face Greg Maddux, who came dangerously close to no-hitting the Tribe in Game 1.

The best spin Hargrove could conjure up was, "It's not the most pleasant prospect, but there are 26 teams sitting at home right now who would like to be in our place."

So true, but the Indians playing in the World Series were not the same Indians who had won 100 games in the regular season. The boom in the bats had been mostly thuds. Hershiser, Hill and Martinez could have combined for a class-action suit against the hitters, charging them with non-support, and every court in northern Ohio would have found in their favor.

"Sometimes you just have to say that the other team deserves credit," Hargrove said. "The Braves have the best pitching in baseball. You have to tip your hat to them."

That was true, but there was something else going on, too.

To beat Atlanta, the Indians needed to play championship baseball. They needed to run the bases like they knew what they were doing. They needed to catch the ball and they needed to pay attention to where they were throwing it. Sure, they had been doing those things better than any

Indians team in the last 30-some years, but the Indians also had stepped up in class. To win the World Series, they just had to play better than they did.

Then came Game 5. And for one more night, this was a championship team.

The Indians played Game 5 of the World Series like they had played 100 of them in the regular season. They hit the ball a mile. They kicked it around a little bit, and they were picked off base. That was the 1995 Indians: power bats, power arms and bizarre base-running. Their 5-4 victory over Atlanta was was one more dose of Indians Summer.

Horns were blasting on the streets of the city, which seemed to come to life, riding the waves of the best baseball team since 1948. Thirty minutes after the game, about 5,000 fans were still at Jacobs Field, all behind the Tribe's dugout just so they could catch a glimpse of the players who were returning to the field to do some TV interviews.

This was the team that was 100-44 and won the Central Division by 30 games. This was the team for which Jim Thome hit a 436-foot homer to dead center that flew into the night, "like a homesick angel," to quote Tribe great Bob Feller, who watched it from the press box.

The game wasn't supposed to turn out this way. The Indians had to face this decade's greatest pitcher in Greg Maddux, who had stuffed their bats in Game 1 in Atlanta.

"No one gave us a chance," said catcher Sandy Alomar. "I mean, they had their ace pitching. One more loss and we go home. We just weren't ready to go home."

Before the game, Tribe starter Orel Hershiser noticed that the players were asking each other for autographs.

"It was an unspoken thing — like we need to sign these things today because there may not be another day," he said. "Greg Maddux is the toughest opponent you can face — at this time, even in this century. The mountain was real high to climb. But our offense knows how to adjust. They talked with each other. They studied film. They did not want to be the same team they were in Game 1."

The Indians dug their spikes into the dirt at home plate, squirted tobacco juice, and dared Maddux to knock them out.

Not in our house. That was the message.

In the first inning, Maddux fired a fastball under Eddie Murray's chin. It nearly tore Murray's head off, and it came exactly one pitch after

Albert Belle put a line drive in the right-field bullpen for a two-run homer. Murray yelled at Maddux. The benches emptied. No punches were thrown, but Hershiser sought out the Braves pitcher.

"Did you throw at him?" he asked Maddux.

"No, I just wanted to jam him," Maddux replied.

"Well, you're better than that," Hershiser said.

Then Hershiser said, "You know, I have the ball, too."

The threat was clear: Hershiser was ready, willing and able to deck any one of their hitters — at any time. He didn't. There was no need. Maddux never threw at anyone again during the game because he knew that Hershiser was called "The Bulldog" during his Dodger days. Hershiser could put a snarl on his face and bite hard with his fastball. Maddux knew that Hershiser was a devout Christian, but he also knew that Jesus threw the money-changers out of the temple.

Hershiser would not allow his hitters to be bullied. He allowed them to live for one more trip to Atlanta.

But that was all there would be — one more game.

The Indians could manage only one hit in Game 6, losing 1-0 to Tom Glavine. For the six-game series, the Indians batted only .179 and averaged three runs per game — this from a team that hit .291 and scored six runs a game during the regular season.

But, really, this wasn't that hard for me to accept. Yes, the Indians won more games in the regular season — thereby making them the best team in baseball in sheer numbers — but the Braves were superior in terms of experience and pitching. They played smarter and simply pitched better. They had been to the World Series three times in this decade. They had paid more dues, suffered more setbacks. And it showed.

Maybe that was why I wasn't very disappointed when it was over.

The next morning as I was fighting the World Series blues, I found myself staring out of a jet window while my flight circled Cleveland. I saw Jacobs Field and the old Stadium. I saw Cleveland State and the Galleria. I saw the city where I grew up and I thought, "It's better now than I remember."

How often can we say that about anything?

The Cleveland of my youth was a great place to get a tattoo. It was a dirty lake and a flammable river. It was the worst ballpark in the major leagues. It was a city of streets you wouldn't walk down at night without a pit bull and an Uzi. The reason the old Cleveland jokes of the 1960s and

1970s hurt so bad is because so much of what was said was true.

I will not hear any argument on this. I've lived on both sides of town. Now that the future is bright, I will not allow any revisionist history of the bleak past.

I grew up with the Indians. I loved them, but they fit right in with the town; they were another Cleveland embarrassment. They were the Indians of Frank Lane, who traded Rocky Colavito and Roger Maris. They were the Indians of Jack Kralick and Gary Bell, who once had a fistfight over what to watch on TV — and that was back before cable, when there were only three channels.

These Indians had the Beer Night Riot, and they passed out deodorant to women on Mother's Day. These Indians had Tony Horton's mental breakdown, Herb Score's eye injury and Sam McDowell. Ah yes, Sudden Sam, who broke two ribs on his first pitch for the Tribe and then broke everyone's heart with his promise lost at the bottom of the bottle.

Perhaps you know all these horror stories already and don't want to hear them again. But it is worth remembering what the Indians were and what Cleveland was. It's worth understanding how the team and city have changed.

The fact that most of us waited 20, 30 and even 40 years for a World Series, the fact we still cared about this baseball team while so much time passed with so little to show for it — that should make you treasure this 1995 model even more.

I thought about Mike Hargrove, who was second-guessed in the World Series. Hey, even I second-guessed him, and I bet he did a few things that he wouldn't mind trying over.

This season was a tribute to Hargrove. He and his wife Sharon and their five children invested 14 years of their lives in this team. Hargrove played for the Indians, he managed at every level of the team's farm system, and then he became the first manager in 41 years to deliver a pennant.

Never forget that.

Despite his sometimes questionable moves, there was only one way Hargrove could have won the 1995 World Series. He would have had to grab a bat and do what Albert Belle and the boys could not do: hit the best pitching in baseball.

Don't forget that, either.

The 1995 Indians were a talented team. But Manny Ramirez couldn't always remember the count. Kenny Lofton could be hypersensitive and withdrawn. Jim Thome was baseball's Forrest Gump. Paul Sorrento grumbled about not playing against left-handed pitchers when he often couldn't hit righties.

There was more.

Sandy Alomar was constantly fighting injuries and Dennis Martinez was battling Father Time. Charles Nagy could be riddled with self-doubt. Alvaro Espinoza had to be reminded to leave the tacos and beans alone, because he had a habit of growing bloated while sitting on the bench.

Then there was Albert Belle. Hargrove was the first manager who did not have to suspend the volcano in left field, and Belle became a superstar while on Hargrove's watch.

Managing these Indians required a steady hand, a thick hide and a quick head. In the fall of 1995, Hargrove was 46, still a relatively young manager in terms of age and experience. During his next post-season run, he will handle some things differently — as will the Indians.

I wasn't on the Tribe's charter flight, which landed at 3 a.m. at Cleveland Hopkins International Airport, but what I heard about the Indians, who had just lost the World Series, made me feel even better about this team.

The fans were kept about 75 yards away behind a fence. The players could have gone straight from the airplane to the bus, dismissing the fans with a quick wave. But Hargrove led the team for a long walk along that fence. They touched the fans' fingers through the fence, said hello, and let the thousands who had shown up in the middle of the night get a close look at them.

Hargrove knew the moment. He knew the fans, and he knew his players. He did what you'd want the manager of your baseball team to do — he acted like a decent human being who cared about the folks who pay the freight.

Growing up with the Indians, I had no memories like that heroes' welcome — although I am sure that my father would have taken me to the airport to see this great team had it played back in the 1960s. It would have been special to him because he knew what it would have meant to me, his young son.

Imagine being a kid today — a baseball fan. Think about growing up with the 1995 Indians as your boys of summer. Imagine the stories you'll have to tell your children.

Belle-Baerga-Lofton.

Those three names will become one word, rolling off the lips of fans just as Wynn-Lemon-Feller-Garcia came from the mouths of our parents and grandparents.

You'll be able to talk about how 40-year-old Dennis Martinez threw the game of his life, beating Randy Johnson in Seattle's Kingdome to put the Tribe in the World Series.

"I never, ever, will forget that game," Martinez said. "I just hope that the Cleveland fans will remember it, too."

Don't worry, Dennis, the fans will remember that you made history.

Today's kids will tell tomorrow's children about Orel Hershiser's grit, Albert Belle's fire, Omar Vizquel's grace and Kenny Lofton's legs.

They'll have stories about a wonderful park where all the restrooms worked.

This Indians team did more than win the American League pennant. It created a new generation of Cleveland baseball fans whose memories will be much better than ours.

About The Author:

Burying The Curse is Terry Pluto's 15th book, and it's a sequel to *The Curse of Rocky Colavito*, which was named one of the five notable sports books of 1994 by the New York Times. *Loose Balls*, his story of the old American Basketball Association, was named the best sports book of 1990 by USA Today. Pluto's newest basketball book is *Falling From Grace*, an inside look at the NBA in the voices of its players, coaches and general managers. Pluto has been with the Akron Beacon Journal since 1985. He is a three-time Ohio Sportswriter of the Year and was nominated for the 1994 Pulitzer Prize for commentary.